an Adventure Begins

To Martin
Enjoy the journey!
Alana

Sailing to Skye
an Adventure Begins

Alana Parker

© Alana Parker 2011

Published by Little Boat Publishing

ISBN 978-0-9568201-0-5

All Rights Reserved. No part of this book may be reproduced, adapted, stored in a retrieval system or transmitted by any means, electronic, mechanical, photocopying, or otherwise without the prior written permission of the author.

Cover design by Liv Cawston

Prepared and printed by:

York Publishing Services Ltd
64 Hallfield Road
Layerthorpe
York YO31 7ZQ

Tel: 01904 431213

Website: www.yps-publishing.co.uk

Table of Contents

A New Adventure Begins	1
Scarborough to Peterhead	18
Peterhead to Inverness	27
The Caledonian Canal	32
Fort William to Oban	44
Oban to Tobermory	53
Isle of Mull to Isle of Skye	59
Return to the Caledonian	74
Inverness to Stonehaven	93
Stonehaven to Blythe	114
The Homeward Leg	123
Postscript	128

A New Adventure Begins

"Head her into the wind – I have to get the main down before we're flattened!" This was Steve's voice desperately trying to be heard over the wind. "I can't – we'll have to run for shelter to do that". As I said this I wondered if we could make it – the storm was whipping up and I was sure it was force 7 by now, though there was no way I could stop to check this with the wind gauge. We were out in open sea crossing the Cuillin Sound, having left the Isle of Skye and heading for the Canna Straits. The storm was coming straight from the Atlantic Ocean.

By now the jib, that we had optimistically hanked-on to the forestay before we left our sheltered mooring on Skye, was waving frantically about in the strong gusts, and Steve battled his way to the bow where he manfully wrestled with the billowing sailcloth, then somehow brought it back to the cockpit to stow below. I, on the helm, was petrified that I might not hold her steady, that an almighty surge of wind and waves would force the rudder out of my grip and Steve would be overboard! That thought was quickly forced aside and I gripped the stick even tighter, knowing if that happened I would be the only one there to save him – and that meant stopping the boat – this bucking bronco that was being tossed across the sea by the force of nature in its angriest of states! Not only would I have to stop the boat, but also the sail would have to be taken down, and I would have to turn the boat around and find him – not to mention the problem of getting him back aboard. Of course safety & rescue procedures had been discussed in the comfort of our cosy saloon below, moored-up safely in the harbour: but that was a far cry from the conditions we now faced.

With wave heights reaching 3-4meters our 29ft yacht Grautvornix was being hurled up each wall of water and was surfing down the other side, only to start the manoeuvre over again. We made it through the straits between Canna & Rum and turned her head into the wind behind the island – but the wind deceived us! It was blowing around this huge lump of rock that towers menacingly out of the water, and coming at us from both sides. We went in as close as we dare, to get some lee, and I put the engine on full revs to hold her head into the wind. Steve was at the mast ready to pull down the mainsail. She was straining to turn as the wind blew even harder, and I held onto the helm with one hand, revving the engine to keep her steady – all the time watching the rocks of Rum that were too close for comfort.

The fierceness of the storm had not been predicted – we had listened to the shipping forecast the night before and knew it would be fresh – force 4/5 – but there had been no indication of this. We had set off down the calm waters of Loch Harport at 05.00hrs to get the tide in our favour, had hoisted the full main, with the intention of putting in a reef or two as the wind freshened. The jib was hanked-on and fastened down on the foredeck, ready to be hoisted if needed. We wore our all-weather gear and lifejackets, stowed everything safely below, made sandwiches as "grab" food for the voyage, and considered ourselves well prepared.

At this moment I thought of a conversation we had had during the planning of our month-long sailing trip from our home town of Scarborough on the North East coast of England to the Isle of Skye, Scotland. "We can take our time, and we don't have to go out in any bad weather," said Steve, reassuringly, "we will just stay put wherever we are, if the conditions aren't right for us". Foolishly I had believed this.

Perhaps I should introduce us: I am a fifty-something lady who actually thinks she is much younger than that. In fact I get a shock each time I spot my reflection because in my mind my skin is much smoother and my hair has no grey roots at all (which by the way it does not, immediately after my hairdresser had been paid handsomely to colour it). I am pretty healthy and fit enough to fling myself about the deck of a yacht at the beck and call of my skipper. My skipper is also, I'm happy to say, my husband Steve. Steve is also fifty-something and an engineer, a trade whose skills are greatly to be desired aboard a boat. I am an accountant, a trade whose skills are of very little use on a boat. However, I do have some useful attributes: I'm a good cook, very important to a boat's crew, and I have loads of patience – essential when dealing with most boat skippers. Steve is a hard taskmaster and demands perfection of himself and his crew, and is completely intolerant of fools. We make a good team and although we haven't a huge amount of sailing experience, we work well together and somehow manage to get our little yacht, Grautvornix, to perform well enough. We compliment each other – that's the secret. By that I don't mean we spend our time saying "Ooh you're so clever" or "You did that perfectly"! I mean that where one of us has a weakness, the other has strength and vice-versa.

Together Steve and I have shared many adventures and challenges, somehow always managing to retain the utmost respect for each other, and this summer's sailing trip to the Isle of Skye was to be yet another one. Now back to the story.

We had been in Scarborough Yacht Club sitting at the bar enjoying a beer and the company of fellow sailing members, when Steve said to me "you know, I don't think I'll do the North Sea Race next year – let's do something different: why don't you & I sail the boat up to the west coast of Scotland?" Now this sounded good to me, for a couple of reasons. One: I don't like racing (not competitive by nature) Two: I love the west coast of Scotland (with a passion). The plan was hatched and we began to build on it with ideas on the when, where & how etc. We needed to get the time off work, as we estimated the whole trip would need a month, to allow us time for delays due to weather or repairs etc. July would be the month, because this was (a) the best weather window & (b) the club's North

Sea Race (so Steve wouldn't be missing anything back at the club!) That was the "when" settled – next came the "where". The farthest we had sailed to date was the island of Mull – we had taken our previous boat, Windrift, a Contessa 26 up there a few years previously – and so the next challenge had to be the Isle of Skye.

The outbound trip would take us from our homeport to Inverness, via Peterhead, Whitehills and Lossiemouth. We drew a straight line from Scarborough to Peterhead and said "we can do this in one long overnight haul". Ahem. That was me reminding Steve that, although he is an excellent sailor, his first mate (i.e. me) was not so confident as a sailor. This is where good crew come in – and Russ was as keen as mustard to be involved. So it was decided the two of us would become three – for the first leg that is. Once we reached Inverness, the entry to the Caledonian Canal, Russ would take the train back home and leave us to it.

Through the canal would take us three days, negotiating all the locks, and we would emerge out onto the west coast with a whoop and a holler, so to speak. Oban would be our first port, then up to Tobermory on Mull, a diversion up Loch Sunart (we both just fancied it) and onto the Isle of Skye, our target destination.

The months came and went while Steve busied himself with all the jobs required to make Grautvornix ready for the big trip.

As I said earlier, our previous boat (and our first yacht) was a Contessa 26 that we had bought from a fellow yacht club member, and knew to be a well-maintained craft; She was solid and reliable, or, as I liked to think of it, very forgiving. This seemed just what we needed, never having sailed before, and therefore expecting to make many mistakes. We had both been scuba divers for many years, which is how we met, and had plenty of experience of the sea, but no knowledge of sails and how to use them. We joined the local yacht club and were quickly welcomed into the yachty scene, there being no shortage of experienced sailors here; we were taken out and shown the basics. Steve already had his yacht master qualification (for motor boats) and I spent the winter studying the rules of the sea and navigation skills, in the RYA Day Skipper night class run by one of our club's members.

Finally we acquired Windrift – named Llamados by her previous owner whose general attitude can be gleaned from reading the name backwards – and took her out to sea. All went reasonably well on our first venture out of the harbour and around the bay, but one day we took her a little further – sailing to the North (or Norad as the locals refer to it) we were really getting up some speed and were ecstatic with our progress. The wind was fresh and southerly, blowing our little boat along with great gusto. Then we turned for home, gibing her around as we'd been instructed, and set off southwards (Suthad in the Northerner's language) – or tried to. The wind now was not performing the way we wanted it to! The sails flapped alarmingly and the boat came to a standstill – we tacked and gibed, backwards and forwards, trying to catch some wind to propel us forward, but achieving only a few yards before we had to perform the manoeuvre yet again – this was hopeless! The tide by now had turned and we had to put the engine on to beat against it and the wind, now blowing directly at us. We arrived back in the harbour, eventually, feeling battered, wet and cold and thoroughly exhausted. As we approached our boat cradle, our immediate neighbour, a sprightly man well into his 70s who had been sailing all his life, shouted, "what a fantastic day for sailing – I'm just going out!" It was then we realised we were missing something...

We had four years of learning to sail on Windrift and eventually decided that we really wanted to do some serious cruising and for that we needed a different boat. My specifications for the boat were as follows: "she must be big enough for me to stand up in and have a separate cabin to sleep in". Steve's specifications were a little more technical!

Once we had decided that the Hanse 291 was the boat we wanted, we initially searched the UK agencies and then started to look further as the prices seemed too high. At the time the pound was still quite strong against the Euro and the prices in Holland and Germany were considerably lower, so we took a cheap flight across to Amsterdam and hired a car to go around a couple of boatyards. Taking photographs of each boat from all angles, we returned home to consider them. In the meantime we were also looking at some of the German boat agencies and Steve spotted Grautvornix berthed in Laboe, Kiel Bay. We got in touch and arranged to be collected from Hamburg airport by the agent, who would then drive us to view the boat, later delivering us back to the city. It worked extremely well and we had a wonderful evening in Hamburg, before catching our return flight the following day. As soon as we stepped onto Grautvornix we both knew she was the boat for us. What excited us was the fact that her one-owner had tampered with nothing. Everything was original and had been lovingly maintained. The interior was immaculate and I imagined Herr Pruss being very strict with anyone who came aboard. In fact I was proved correct when we later came to collect her.

At this point I should perhaps enlighten you about the origins of the boat's name. As I said, we bought her in Germany from a man who was as fastidious as a German should be, and had kept Grautvornix in perfect condition. To be fair, though, she had sailed only in the calm inland waters of the Elbe and rarely, if ever, ventured out into the harsh conditions of the North Sea. She was built by Hanse in 1997, has a sloop rig and an overall length of 9 metres. Herr Pruss had bought her when she was new and named her Grautvornix after a character in the comic book Asterix (as he did all his previous boats apparently), which roughly translates as "Fears Nothing". We intended to change the name, but to be honest it was a real conversation piece wherever we went, so Grautvornix it was.

When the day came to sign the paperwork and collect the boat we were in a state of great excitement. We had gathered together a crew of three of our very good friends to help Steve sail Grautvornix back across the North Sea:

Tom – the local lifeboat coxswain, diver of many years experience and carpenter extraordinaire.

Arthur – diver of many years (in the old days when spear-fishing was allowed!), experienced single-handed ocean-going sailor and retired college lecturer.

Mick – diver, cyclist, water-sports fanatic and IT specialist.

We planned to hire a minibus and drive/ferry/drive across to Laboe. I would be the driver – which was a bit disappointing as I didn't get to sail back, but as Steve said: "The driver is a very important part of the mission – and you will get plenty of opportunity to sail later" He omitted to add: "and of course I really want this to be a boys' adventure too!" There was great excitement as we loaded all our bags into the hire vehicle – and there was a lot of luggage: four sets of wet-weather gear, sleeping bags, provisions, safety gear etc. etc. We drove down to Hull and boarded the over-night ferry in very high spirits. After a meal on board, and a couple of beers to help us sleep, we retired to our cabins, waking early the next morning to the usual "Boing! Boing! Goede morgen dames en herren" as we were welcomed into the port of Rotterdam. After a good breakfast we all piled back into the minibus and prepared to leave the ferry. It was a really hot sunny day in June 2006 as I drove through Holland and across the German border. We headed towards Osnabruck, turned north for Bremen, skirted around Hamburg, on and on towards Kiel, finally hitting the coast and Laboe. Whew! What a journey – and I had it all to do again – alone!

We met the agent and the owner Her Pruss, completed the paperwork, shook hands on the deal and went straight off down to the pontoons to board our new boat. Herr Pruss had agreed to go out on the water with us to "show us the ropes" as they say and of course to give the crew some helpful advice about the boat. As I mentioned earlier, he was most particular, to the point of actually shouting at the crew once or twice when one of them handled something a little carelessly. Soon, however, he was off the boat and Steve became the rightful owner and skipper.

Later we headed off to a café on the waterfront for a meal. It was Saturday and very busy but we managed to get a table outside in the sunshine, where I noticed everyone staring at us. Either they were not used to seeing English tourists in that area, or they were bemused by the crew shirts that we all wore – emblazoned with the boat's name and with the Asterix character embroidered underneath. It wasn't until much later I discovered that it was the wrong character! Asterix is very big in Europe and everyone would have known it was not Grautvornix. However, at the time we thought we all looked like a proper crew and were "gung ho" about it.

After the meal, we all made ready to board the boat and get a good night's sleep in readiness for the big adventure we all had ahead of us.

The alarm went just before 07.00hrs on Sunday and I had to say goodbye at this point, as I was due back in Rotterdam that evening for the return ferry. I said my goodbyes and as I did I felt proud of my husband and our friends as they slipped the mooring ropes and motored away in a strange boat down an unfamiliar waterway, en route to the open sea.

As I drove confidently out of the town, towards the motorway, I was horrified to see "Motorway Closed" signs posted at the "Eingang" slipway. What on earth was going on? Where do I go now? I doubled-back on myself and drove towards the motorway once again, just in case I had misunderstood, or in any case to give myself time to think. Yes it was indeed closed, and now I could see the maintenance-men working on it – that section was to be closed until Sunday night. The Germans don't mess about – "if work needs doing then we close it!" I found another road that ran alongside the motorway and joined it later. What I didn't realise was that, whilst I was having this problem, Steve was having his own personal crisis:

"Where the hell is my passport?!" he was shouting to anyone who would listen. He answered himself shortly after that. "Oh, no! It's in Alana's handbag!" He rang my mobile – I didn't have it switched on while driving. The rest of the long journey went well for me, oblivious as I was to the passport problem. I made the ferry port on time and had no problems with the minibus, so I was quite happy as I had dinner on board and prepared for an early night. I slept really well after the long day.

The crew meanwhile were experiencing all the stress that accompanies sailing a boat for the first time down a canal you've never seen before, with the prospect of popping out the other end into the North Sea and all the perils that can bring. Steve's train of thought was something like this: "Right, we're in German water, we're flying an Ensign and a German courtesy flag on the spreader and I have no passport. Let's just hope the authorities don't decide to inspect us." As it happens, they didn't. Grautvornix made her way down the canal, passing the German pub where they watch all the boats and play the appropriate national anthem for them as they pass, through the lock and out into the

North Sea with no incidents. The weather was fair, the wind light and the passage was already in the plotter – only 300 miles to go!

By the time they sailed into Scarborough harbour on Wednesday afternoon I was waiting on the East Wall watching them arrive. The passage had been slow due to the light winds, but the boys had all enjoyed the experience and Arthur had kept them entertained with all his many stories.

Back to our trip preparations: Steve is a perfectionist, and because of this, he now spent every spare moment working on preparing Grautvornix for the big trip. The Volvo engine had to be overhauled and tested. The sails were inspected in great detail – the racing sails would be taken off to preserve their performance – and the cruising chute added to the sail locker, which we would use in place of the large racing spinnaker. Sheets and halyards were all checked and replaced, where necessary. A pair of white dodgers was fastened to the guardrails each side of the cockpit and the spray hood attached (all these add to the comfort of cruising by keeping me dry!). The auto-helm came out of its box and was calibrated, in anticipation of some reasonable conditions during the longer passages – freeing-up the crew to do other things. Extra fenders were stowed and the basket of mooring warps was full to overflowing. The standard anchor was replaced with a much more robust CQR, complete with chain anchor cable. The life raft and the inflatable rubber tender were both brought out of the shed and checked over – the tender proved to have a small leak, which Steve sealed with glue and tape (an ineffective repair, as we were later to discover!). The radar reflector was replaced with a more effective (and consequently more expensive!) version because we had heard the story of the yacht that was run-down by a passing freight ship that couldn't see her on the radar, with the loss of all aboard.

Navigation equipment came next – the GPS had to be loaded with the charts required for the area we would be visiting. Once we had established our route, this was put into the GPS by marking the waypoints. We had decided on plans A & B, and these would be taking account of the weather and sea conditions. Plan A would see us sailing a long first leg from Scarborough to Peterhead, some 200 nautical miles, which would take us approximately 34 hours including an overnight, and it was reasonable to assume we would not want to do this in rough weather. Plan B would take us to Blythe and Eyemouth for overnight stops, arriving in Peterhead on Day 3. Two Passage Plans were then drawn-up and distances and passage times worked out, taking account of tidal information, and the various port entry details, which were extracted from the invaluable Reeds Almanac. At last it was all coming together – we had a plan!

Now, I don't quite remember how it came about, but Steve discovered the Classic Malts Whisky Cruise. We are both fans of a classic malt or two and have tasted many a good dram on our dive trips around the Scottish islands, visiting many of the distilleries on the islands as we passed by. We have a good friend in Germany who prides himself on being able to name all of the Islay Malts and have spent many a night with

Roger discussing the delights and nuances of these wonderful Scottish whiskies. Bear with me a moment whilst I reminisce over our holiday spent on Islay several years previously. We had arranged to go for a week of diving and Malts tasting (not at the same time!) with two of our diving buddies, who shared our love of the Scottish amber nectar. They had a small RIB (Rigid Inflatable Boat – like a dinghy but with a rigid hull) and we loaded all our diving gear into Rob's van and hitched the boat to his tow bar. It was August and I was looking forward to a lovely summer's week away from everything. We certainly were away from everything – the cottage we had booked was in the middle if the island, surrounded only by farmland – bliss, you would think. The truth is that the weather that week was more suited to November than August and the sea, where we would do our diving of course, was as far away as you can get on an island. So every day we got up from our very cold beds (did I mention the cottage was damp and freezing?) dressed in our diving undersuits – which I was very glad of, as they are cosy-warm – and drove across the windswept island to the coast. Launching the RIB was a daily challenge. Rob had done his homework and knew where the wrecks were, but there was not always a suitable launch-site close by, so we often had to improvise – by that I mean we had to manhandle the boat into the water from the closest thing we could find to a "slip". Sometimes we were lucky and located a beach where we could drive the trailer down to the water's edge. The water was beautifully clear and once we had located the wrecks with the aid of the GPS the diving was magical.

The kelp forests were swirling back and forth in the current, bright green and shiny brown, hiding all manner of fish and crustaceans. The wreckage of the unfortunate shipping that succumbed to the relentless weather and tides on the exposed side of the island was pretty-well broken up, but we enjoyed finning around, trying to identify the various bits that remained. After our day's diving we would retrieve the boat and fasten it securely back onto the trailer, driving back to our cold cottage to shower and change before heading off again to find a nice pub and a hot meal. In-between diving we took the opportunity of visiting some of the famous distilleries – always a pleasure! On the last day the weather was even worse than it had been the rest of the week. We managed one final dive before we had to load everything up again for the homeward journey. I felt happy but exhausted as we finally arrived at Port Ellen to await the ferry that would take us across to Tarbert, from where we would begin the 7-hour drive home. It transpired that the next ferry would not arrive for another 2 hours, and looking around I was relieved to see a homely-looking café: "Oh great!" I exclaimed, "We can get hot chocolates and toasted tea-cakes!" however Rob had other ideas. Did I mention that Rob was a restless soul who has to fill every minute with an adventure of some sort? "We've got time for another dive – this ferry pier could hide all manner of treasures! Let's get the boat launched!" Standing there in the cold pouring rain, my hair whipping my face in the wind, with all our bags packed and the smell of hot coffee wafting across the air, I couldn't think of anything I wanted to do less than strip off, don diving gear, and jump into that icy water. Rob seemed most surprised at this.

The Scottish Malts Cruise was taking place in July of 2009 and this is exactly when we planned to be in the area – we went onto the website and found that the three meeting points were the distilleries in Oban, on the west coast of mainland Scotland, Carbost, on the Isle of Skye where the Talisker is distilled, and the Lagavulin distillery on Islay. The cruise is very popular and boats arrive from all over Europe to join in – we heard from a very well-travelled Dutch skipper that the west coast of Scotland is considered "the best cruising ground in the whole of Europe". I can truly believe that. We paid our subscription and became a part of it.

Our intention was to build the Cruise into our itinerary, joining-up with them in Oban for the start of the event, and on the Isle of Skye for the second meeting. We reluctantly accepted that we wouldn't make the Islay date due to time constraints. We had only a month, and although that sounds a long time, the journey to and from the west coast would take up half of it. I was beginning to get excited now, and we ordered 2 Classic Malts Cruise crew shirts to get us into the spirit of it.

My mind now turned to preparations for living aboard the boat for a month –for the first week there would be three aboard – and the equipment we would need plus the general "vittleing up". For the first leg I would prepare a large pan of a one-pot meal that could be easily heated-up and eaten out of a bowl with just a fork or spoon. I chose a pasta dish for this, as it is both filling and nutritious, not to mention tasty. I would make it in my trusty old pressure cooker (the kind everyone of a certain age has at the back of a cupboard somewhere) as this has a secure lid to keep the contents safe during the trip. Then we would need lots of "grab food" for the long first leg – that is biscuits, chocolate, cereal bars, crisps & fruit etc. Basic food & drink items for later in the trip we could stow away under the bunks – with a few beers left out for celebrating our arrival in Peterhead (I knew we would be feeling exhausted but exhilarated after a long haul). We would have to plan clothing for all weathers – the British climate is so unpredictable, especially out at sea, and knowing Scotland as we did, anything from winter to summer weather could be expected, even if it is July! Our Musto All-Weather Gear, fleeces, life jackets, safety harnesses and sea boots were all put aboard, together with our shorts, sun glasses, sun cream and sun hats. Bedding – I insisted on taking my nice duvet & pillows, for I was determined to be as comfortable as possible – plus sleeping bags for catnaps on the overnight passages.

After months of planning, the eve of our departure date eventually dawned and it was time to stow everything. We loaded the car with our bags of clothes & provisions and final bits of equipment. Our friend and crewman, Russ, met us at the marina with his kit bag and an excited smile, to help load-up the boat. I confirmed arrangements to pick him up in the car the following morning at 3am so that we could sail out of the harbour on the morning tide.

Scarborough to Peterhead

The alarm sounded at 2am and we both were immediately awake – the excitement and apprehension running in equal measures. A quick cup of coffee and a last minute check around the house, and we were off on our adventure. I dropped Steve off at the harbour and drove the 5 miles to where Russ lived, and he was waiting on the pavement with an impatient look on his face. He just wanted to be off!

The weather was a little cloudy, with a light easterly breeze and as we motored out of the harbour mouth, I thought how strange it was to be leaving our homeport for a whole month. I thought of our children – all old enough to be independent of us – but still I wondered if they'd all be all right without us for the month. I know – can't help it, it's just a "mother" thing. Steve would give me one of his looks, if I mentioned this, so I didn't.

We motored out of the South Bay and around the castle headland into the North Bay, enjoying the peace of the dawn, each with our own thoughts, when the engine sound changed. We all looked at each other –

we couldn't believe it! The engine was overheating and we hadn't got out of Scarborough's water yet! Steve took the engine box off and his head disappeared into the engine housing (a place I try never to go – except to turn the batteries on or off). Half an hour of Steve & Russ doing engine checks and discussing the why & the wherefore, and we were off again – all wondering if this was a good start to our long journey.

The sun came up and a beautiful day dawned as we passed the familiar landmarks along our North Eastern coastline, sometimes referred to as the Dinosaur Coast. Ravenscar, where one of our dive-club members (turned archaeologist) found a real dinosaur footprint, now proudly displayed in the Rotunda Museum in Scarborough. Robin Hood's Bay, a natural bay cut by the sea and a popular site for "toffee-hammer tappers", as I like to call the amateur archaeologists, looking for fossils. It also has a wreck in the bay that is a very popular dive-site, and is known locally for having its own microclimate. We have crossed the bay many times in various boats on what was everywhere else a smooth sea, only to be tossed around like a cork by "The Bay's" personal storm in progress. Runswick Bay, a favourite of mine & Steve's, where we often go walking and nearly always end up in The George, a cosy traditional-style pub with a log fire. I remembered, as we sailed passed, one occasion when we took our friends who were visiting from Germany to the George one Christmas, because we had bought several tickets for the annual Draw. Liz & Roger joined-in with the general joyful atmosphere and after several drinks and a few more tickets bought, the Draw was made. To our amazement Liz & Roger won a brace of Pheasants! They obviously couldn't take them home with them, and being vegetarian myself I wasn't keen, so they presented my mother with the brace, much to her delight.

On board Grautvornix, we all sat in silence, just taking-in the views and the smell of the sea, each of us thinking how lucky we were. The last land we sited was Whitby, with its mysterious Abbey atop the cliff, and its association with the "Goths" who frequent the town. The shoreline then turns away to the west and our course took us north, away into the open sea on course for Scotland. At 09.00hrs the wind picked up and we hoisted the Jib and were sailing along joyously at about 5.5 knots from then until 15.00hrs when the wind died away and we had to put the engine on. From then on we motor-sailed the rest of the day and night – the sea was now oily-flat with no wind at all. The sky was cloud –covered with no stars to be seen, but we didn't need them for light, as the night never really seemed to get dark, being the height of summer. We organised a system of watches, from 22.00hrs onwards, so that we were each on the helm for 2 hours, sleeping for 2 hours and on stand-by for 2 hours. Being on stand-by meant you were available to make hot drinks, snacks etc and to keep watch for other shipping, but you could doze in the corner of the cockpit if you wanted. We attached the Auto-helm to the tiller, which was not altogether successful as we were still having problems with it "dropping-out" every now & then. You couldn't leave it as it would suddenly beep at you and you constantly had to re-set the bearing. It was a nuisance, but at least you didn't have to hold onto the tiller all the time, which could be quite tiring.

At midnight I had just slid thankfully into my sleeping bag, when the engine alarm sounded – I sat bolt upright, not knowing what it meant, and found Steve re-fuelling. It took 20 litres of fuel and Steve by now was very concerned about the engine.

I fell into a deep sleep after that and was awoken yet again by a very loud alarm that was indeed alarming! I had no idea what it was – and this time I knew it was something serious. I shot out of the cabin into the cockpit to see Russ & Steve both looking alarmed (pardon the pun) – then we all heard "Pan Pan, Pan Pan" come over the VHF – apparently there had been a distress flare sighted over Aberdeen and we received a DSC (Digital Selective Calling) distress alert over the VHF, which we hadn't ever encountered before. What a relief that was! We were nowhere in the vicinity of Aberdeen, so couldn't assist, and we all relaxed again. I went off to my bunk feeling not a little cheesed-off that my precious 2 hours sleep had now been twice interrupted.

At 0200hrs I was up again and on standby, with Russ on the helm and Steve going below for much-needed sleep. By 0300hrs the day was again dawning and the gannets were already out on their endless search for fish. During the early hours we were treated to all manner of sea life: porpoises, puffins, guillemots, terns, fulmars, and off the coast of Berwick, a dolphin with pup, which was a delightful sight.

Soon we were passing the Farne Islands – we were too far off shore to see them but we had them on the

GPS plotter – and were visited by many seals, bobbing their heads above the oily-flat surface of the water to see who we were – they are incredibly nosey creatures! Steve & I recalled then the time that we were diving on a reef just off Cayton Bay, near Scarborough, when seals suddenly surrounded us, nipping at our fins and swimming around us. I tried turning round to photograph them but no matter how quick I was they were 10 times faster. I span around in circles, frantically trying to catch sight of them long enough to press the button – they swam like nothing I've ever seen before, and left me quite dizzy.

My favourite by far, though, are the gannets. I have spent many hours at sea watching them fly inches off the sea's surface until they spot a shoal of fish, when they fly high up into the sky, only to plummet down at tremendous speed, and with wings flattened at their sides, they dive headlong into the water. They are perfectly adapted for the task, beautiful in flight and spectacular in dive mode. I could watch them all day. That morning we sighted 7 pairs of them formation flying just above the water, and the sun shining on their brilliant white backs was dazzling.

During the night a racing pigeon had landed on the boat and stayed with us all night, huddled against the side of the coach roof, clearly exhausted. By morning Steve decided it had to go as it was making a mess of his boat: "The damned bird is shitting everywhere!" in his words. He tried his best to make it leave, mostly by throwing it up into the air, but each time it returned, finally choosing the mast spreader as a perch, and staying determinedly out of reach. There it stayed until land was sighted, when it roused itself, shook its wings and took flight, leaving us without a word of thanks!

Before the pigeon's visit our boat had been visited by a swarm of unusual-looking flies – they were quite long-bodied with long wings to match, and slightly reddish in colour. It wasn't that they were harmful to us in any way, just the fact that they arrived in huge numbers. Anything that arrives in a swarm can be a nuisance – and these certainly were. Steve amused himself for several hours with a gadget loaned to us by our friends Dave & Zoe – a racquet-shaped device that was wire criss-crossed & battery-operated. You could swipe the air and catch quite a few at a time – they then "fried" on the wires. Not nice, but it served a purpose and kept Steve amused for hours.

Finally, a rather pretty butterfly arrived aboard, delicately fluttering for a while, and then settling on the starboard side window of the saloon. I called to Steve excitedly, hoping he would share my excitement:

"What next?" he cried "This isn't Noah's bloody Ark!"

Our next changeover was 04.00hrs and shortly before that I noticed Russ having great difficulty staying awake – must have been my scintillating conversation. I told him to get himself off to bed and not to wake Steve for his "stand-by" watch. The weather was still with not a breath of wind (we were on the engine & auto helm) and the sea-state flat calm. There was no other shipping in sight, and there hadn't been all night, so I saw no reason why I could not be left alone for a couple of hours. It would do Steve good to have a good sleep and be fresh for the challenges of the day ahead.

If you think I'm now going to tell you how everything began to go wrong –well you're wrong! I spent the rest of the watch in peace and tranquillity – I even extended it until Steve woke naturally just before 7am feeling refreshed and cheerful (he's dreadful when he hasn't slept, which could have been part of the reason for not waking him!)

As day 2 progressed the wind began to blow, we put up the main and then the Jib and the skipper gave the order to "kill the iron horse!" – not another complaint about the animals – and the engine went quiet. What a lovely sensation; with Russ on the helm we were flying along. All three of us loving the sound of the wind in the sails and the sea whooshing passed as the bow cut through the waves.

The first land we sighted after the long night-passage was Peterhead and we were all three feeling very tired. The harbour entrance is wide and accommodates many large ships, which is why we had to call up the harbour on the VHF radio and request permission to enter. This was granted and we motored into the biggest harbour I've ever encountered. It was straight across to the yacht marina, and we negotiated our way through the much smaller entrance, where, to my surprise, several teenage boys were tearing about on jet skis. The marina is a good size and arranged in a corner of the main harbour, well away from the commercial harbour and just behind the terminal for the oil-industry supply ships. There is a lovely sandy beach around the edge and grassy banks behind that – quite picturesque – as long as you don't look upwards, where a high-security prison is situated. Looking back I have mixed emotions about Peterhead – there were some good encounters, and some quite bad ones.

We moored up on the pontoons and the marina master was soon there to meet us. He gave us a key to the gates and all the information we needed about the facilities. Good Encounter. Steve & Russ got their heads together immediately over the engine overheating problem, whilst I went off towards the garage that we could see in the distance on the hilltop. I had been sent off to buy some gasket glue, and as I approached the garage I noticed it was already closed. Going into the attached "all hours" shop, I enquired about the garage and was directed to an inter-linking door inside the shop. The garage owner was just locking-up so I put on my best "helpless" look and asked if he could possibly sell me some of the sealant. He searched around the workshop and came up with an almost empty tube. I felt sure that wasn't enough and he said all the other tubes would be in the men's tool boxes, which were now all locked as they had left for the weekend. This was bad news because the marina is situated several miles out of town, and with no car and the lateness of the hour, things looked pretty hopeless.

However, and this is the second Good Encounter, the man offered to drive me to the nearest supplier, and not only that, actually waited outside and drove me back to the marina entrance! I was unbelievably grateful, but he refused to take any recompense for his trouble.

Back at the boat Steve & Russ had managed to get all the jobs done and we all went to freshen-up in the marina facilities. These were housed in a small building that also housed the marina office. In front of the building was the most beautiful rockery that was full of colour with beautiful flowers in full bloom. I was most impressed to hear this was the handy- work of the man in charge! After enquiring about eating in the town, we were quite surprised to hear there was only one place to be recommended (that was before we had seen the place). Heading off towards town, we walked around the curve of the sandy beach and up over the grassy banks, onto the road where the Late-Shop was sited. The shop had a double-pricing system, according to when you bought an item (i.e. before 10pm it was one price and was increased to the second price after 10pm). At last we reached the town's main street. I was certainly glad we had asked a local about where to eat in Peterhead, because as we walked around looking for the hotel in question, it became increasingly obvious there really wasn't anywhere else I would have eaten! We were all ravenous by the time we found the place and tucked-into our pub-grub gratefully.

Peterhead to Inverness

We had a leisurely start the next morning as we waited for the tide, leaving Peterhead Marina at 12.00hrs. The weather was warm and sunny with a light Southerly wind – just the right direction for our next passage to Whitehills. We hoisted the main and put up the spinnaker – the wind began to pick-up, and soon we were happily sailing along at 5/6 knots. Passing around Ratray Head we counted ourselves lucky that the weather was fair, having heard some tales about the way the tides rush around that particular headland. Fraserburgh lay ahead, immediately recognisable by the ship wrecked on the rocks and laying half-out of the water.

Whitehills is a small harbour with a very small entrance – again we were lucky with the weather (but not to be so lucky coming into this port on the return journey – more of that later) We arrived at 20.15hrs to find there was only one pub serving meals and that they didn't serve after 8pm – this was not good as there were no shops open either. We decided we didn't need to dress for dinner and rushed straight up the hill to the pub, which is better described as a working-men's-club with its 5 huge TV screens, a pool table and 2 dartboards in one bar. The chef gallantly agreed to "light the pans" for us and we were given a menu with a choice of three items (all with chips of course). Nevertheless, it tasted pretty good after a long day in the open air. At the bar were three men who we knew as the crew of the yacht "Layabout". We had chatted to them in Peterhead and they told us they were retired fishermen who now enjoyed sailing. They had left quite a bit earlier than us, and by the state of them, must have gone straight to the bar on arriving. They were full of "hail fellow well-met" sort of banter, and we tried to politely steer away from them, finding their Scottish brogue had become unintelligible due to the beer with whisky chasers.

Next morning we checked out the Whitehills facilities and found a well-stocked crew-room with comfy chairs and tea, coffee & biscuits, and plenty of books to while away a cold winter's night. The old photos that adorned the walls were of fishing boats and scenes from a bygone era that were fascinating to see. Leaving the small port behind at 10.00hrs we set off towards Lossiemouth, under main and spinnaker and sailed all the way to our destination, passing along the coastline at the Southern side of the Moray Firth. It's a really interesting piece of coastline with many small towns and villages, many of which I had heard of through my links to the fishing industry and I followed them on the GPS plotter with great interest. When back at my office desk I receive many invoices from businesses that service the fishing industry around this area, as I look after the books and records for several fishing companies. Place names like Gamrie Bay, Buckie and Banff have always intrigued me, and here we were sailing past them!

Approaching our next port, Lossiemouth, we had the most amazing spectacle: 18 RAF jets flew out in pairs, straight over our boat and out to sea. The noise was incredible and the sight of those most impressive fighter planes in such numbers was unbelievably exciting. I didn't know our air force was so well equipped!

The weather was changing and we just managed to get the boat jobs done and head for the showers before the wind and rain came through like a wild animal, making us run for the cover of the pub on the corner. The tables in the pub all had charts under the glass and the walls were covered in photographs of local fishing boats, most of them gone now, and photos of the RAF men stationed there. Once again we were famished, and after a welcome pint we headed off to the local Chinese Restaurant that Steve had visited a couple of years earlier. He had whet our appetites with his tales of the Chinese Banquet – so imagine how my heart sank when I saw the sign "closed for re-decoration" on the door.

The three of us walked along the pretty beach promenade and found an Italian Restaurant, where we satisfied our hunger with very mediocre pizzas, before heading back to the boat for an early night.

The result of last night's stormy weather was a very choppy sea, and a Northerly force 4 wind was blowing as we left Lossiemouth the following morning. In full wet-weather gear we motored out into the swell and the surging water around the harbour entrance. A shout from Russ brought our heads round to see a pod of dolphins putting on a show for us as we left – all leaping into the air and splashing back down into the water in the joyous way that dolphins do. As we turned into the wind and hoisted the reefed mainsail, the RAF jets were once again taking off above our heads with a roar that could be heard above the roar of the sea – what a send-off!

We were sailing well this morning and as we hoisted the jib and switched off the engine, the speed increased to 7 knots. With Russ in his element on the helm, I settled into that special corner of the cockpit, where you can tuck yourself away from the wind and just enjoy the ride. Steve worked the winches and trimmed the sails and we were soon watching the Moray Firth narrow-up on the approach to the Kessock Bridge. We had read about the fierce tidal rips at the other side of the bridge, and I was a little apprehensive as we negotiated our way between the bridge piles. I called up Clachnaharry Sea Lock on the VHF and after a short wait at the other side of the river, we were asked to proceed to the lock gates. The lock-keeper was a very jolly rotund man with long hair and Billy Bunter specs (for those of you old enough to remember) who sweated profusely whilst he directed us in his delightful Scottish accent to the marina office.

We tied Grautvornix up securely in Seaport Marina and after registering with the marina office, set off to walk into Inverness. Russ would be leaving us the next day and he wanted to check on the train times. Before we left we greeted the crew of the yacht Layabout, or the "Lazyboys" as Steve had taken to calling them, on their arrival at the marina. The three of us wanted to get a photograph taken in front of the Caledonian Canal sign, which is rather inconveniently sited on the bridge by a very busy road – and it was rush hour, just to add to the difficulties. We spotted a cyclist who had dismounted nearby and hailed him, in order to take said photo. Bad choice. The guy was a nerdy-type who was not content just to hold & press, but wanted to take the ultimate portrait shot, and took a very, very long time over it.

The walk into town took us along the bank of the river Ness and we spotted a very attractive-looking pub where we would return to eat a hearty meal and drink good ale for far longer than was sensible. Well we had to give our crewman a good send-off, didn't we?

The Caledonian Canal

Russ left us at 6am the following morning, nursing a hangover, and went off in the direction of Inverness for his early train. The crew now down to 2, we busied ourselves organising the next stage of our journey. We would take Grautvornix through the Caledonian Canal, via a series of 29 locks, and 4 Lochs (including Loch Ness) and out to the West Coast of Scotland. The first stage was the Muirtown Flight and we were accompanied by several other boats – you find you get chatting to others in the lock whilst you wait for the gates to be opened and closed and the water to fill or empty between the two actions. There was the Margaret M, crewed by 7 old men (I'm not being ageist here – they were all in their 70s!) Then there was the German yacht "Stiefelchen" crewed by a family of three (the teenage daughter later emerged in a purple velour tracksuit to go to the washing facilities). The boat's name translates as "Little Boot" which I found amusing because Boot is also the German word for boat. Being interested in languages myself, I went on to describe to my patiently-listening-husband that the effect of adding the suffix "chen" onto a noun in German renders the item "small" or indeed "cute". For the rest of the trip we adopted this technique, using it at every opportunity – replacing our previous technique of adding "ette" for the same effect i.e. the French version – my own particular favourite being "Bag – ette" meaning a little bag, which now would become "Bag-chen" of course.

Back to the boats in the lock – there was "Bronzie" skippered single-handedly by yet another Steve (he took photos of Grautvornix sailing on Loch Ness and shouted across that he would e-mail them to us – if you see him give him our e-mail address!)

Finally the Lazyboys – yacht "Layabout" – who told us they had to be towed into the Sea Lock by "Miss Marple" (the boat not the intrepid detective), after engine trouble under the Kessock Bridge amid the tidal rips I mentioned earlier. During the rescue their boat's canopy had been ripped, but fortunately no injuries sustained.

Finally through all the locks we emerged into Loch Ness, one of the largest of the Scottish lochs. With the wind directly behind us, we flew the cruising chute, a large billowing bright orange sail, and we were in our element! The weather was gloriously sunny and the scenery every bit as beautiful as the tourist brochure shows it to be. To add to the scene, military helicopters flew either side of the loch, down the length of it, just above our heads, so close that we got a great shot (with the camera not a weapon) and these were quickly followed by military jets on low-flying practice, and an RAF Nimrod marine patrol aircraft with it's easily recognisable nose feature. Just about now our depth gauge registered over 200meters and I felt just a little nervous at the thought of being perched on top of this age-old chasm.

At the far end of Loch Ness lies Fort Augustus, and we moored Grautvornix astern of the Lazyboys, who were all busy mending their canopy. The air was warm and the sun just going down meant that, for the first time, we encountered the dreaded midges. Out came the Deet!

Our good friends Jane & Graham have the supreme good fortune to live in the very pretty village of Fort Augustus – they were at the time taking "time out" of the rat-race and just enjoying life in the Highlands. Some would be envious of them, but I reckon they deserve every minute of it, having seen how hard they worked for many years in a very competitive, cutthroat business. As we waited for them to meet us on the boat, we heard over the VHF that the Lazyboys had called for medical assistance. We watched as they helped one of their crew off the boat, looking as pale as anyone can when they are still alive, and into an ambulance chair that was pushed by the medics along the pontoon to the waiting ambulance. We were subsequently told that he had had an asthma attack, no doubt brought on by their indulgences and the high drama of the sea-rescue.

We walked over to the local pub, "The Bothy", and were shown to one of the few vacant tables. It was of course the height of summer and the place was buzzing with tourists from all over the globe, but being accompanied by well-known locals always helps in this situation. We talked through the meal, the beers flowing, and Steve & I related stories of our travels whilst Graham told us all about the garden shed he was building for himself, with the help of his neighbour, Ray. He had planned it all out carefully, but as is often the case, it had turned into something much more complicated. I couldn't wait to see this shed! The more interesting topic, however, was that of valentine cards. Back in February (the 14th obviously) I had received a valentine card from an anonymous sender, and was at a loss to know who it was. The verse inside had indicated that I knew the person, and that he had red hair. I racked my brain (for a couple of seconds only) and deciding I didn't know anyone with red hair put the card down and thought very little about it. I didn't dwell on it, neither did I stand it up, and the reason for this was my sensitivity towards my husband – he might have imagined there was some dark lover waiting in the wings for me! Fat chance, some might say. Anyway, I now discovered the identity of the sender or senders as it turned out. You may have already guessed that it was Jane and Graham, however I need to explain why. Last winter we had driven up to Fort Augustus to spend a weekend with them, and it had snowed heavily presenting a beautifully white winter scene. We had wanted to go walking, perhaps to climb Ben Nevis, which we knew was a short distance from their house. However Graham had different ideas, and he can be quite persuasive when he wants to be. He desperately wanted to show us Applecross, a small mountain village about an hour away by car, and despite the long car journey we had undertaken to get from Scarborough on the English East Coast to the Scottish West Coast, we agreed to his plan. He had a 4-wheel drive vehicle that was most comfortable and well equipped to cope with the steep snow-clad road that wound steeply upwards towards our destination. The scenery en route was stunning. We took the A87 along the side of Loch Garry, crossing through to Loch Cluanie and passing at the foot of the mountain range known as the Five Sisters and through Glen Shiel. The road followed the eastern bank of Loch Duich to the stunningly beautiful, and much photographed, Eilean Donan Castle, where we headed up the snowy mountainside of Beinn Raimh – stopping on the top to admire the view that was totally white in all directions. A few snowball-fights later and we were back in the car heading down towards Loch Carron, a very pretty village by the loch, where some friends of ours have a holiday home. We stopped to take a photo of their cottage to show them, as it had just been painted and they hadn't been to see it yet. The sun was shining out of a brilliant blue sky and the snow sparkled like a thousand million diamonds as we made our way through the Pass of the Cattle – an amazing single-track road that winds through a series of hairpin bends, with scarily-deep drops to one side, and passing places here and there. The gradient is almost too steep to walk up! Finally descending to Applecross Bay and the pretty village we had come to see. We arrived on the day that the old filling station, whose vintage petrol pumps had been lovingly restored to working order, had been opened amid great ceremony by non-other than Charles Kennedy, former leader of the Lib-Dem party, who it turned out, was the local MP. After a brief look around we went into the pub, whose landlady (disappointingly for me, because it spoiled my romantic idea of the remote Scottish hostelry) was an English woman, already known to our friends as the co-owner of another restaurant. The pub was a complete surprise – after the long drive to this remote spot I was amazed to find the place full to bursting with locals and tourists alike, and who should have pride of place in the middle but Charles Kennedy, his wife and young son. I was fascinated to see such a celebrity in this far-flung place, and as he walked towards us, I smiled and said "hello" to which he replied "Hello, how are you, now?" in a very courteous way. Well Graham was beside himself over this – was I star-struck or something? Why had I smiled at him as if I knew the guy? – I thought it perfectly natural to speak to someone whose face is so well-know throughout the UK, but Graham teased me mercilessly over this. So when February came around, this incident was remembered and my dear friends thought it would be a "hoot" to send me a valentine card from Charles. Only I didn't get it – I got the card all right, but not the joke. They were most disappointed!

Back in Fort Augustus, the following morning, Jane joined us on the boat to take her up the flight of 5 locks, through 2 swing bridges to Loch Oich (I love that name!) and on through the Laggan Locks (2 of them) to Loch Lochy (who thought-up these names?!). As the Loch widened we hoisted the bright orange cruising chute and turned off the engine. With Jane on the helm we sailed out onto the loch. It was not easy controlling the sail as the wind was veering about causing us to steer a very wiggly course, finally being forced to change sails and try the Jib. The wind died away to nothing, and our progress was slow, but the mountains rising up sharply either side of the water gave us stunning scenery all the way down the loch. It was 9th July but the snow still capped the highest peaks.

Meanwhile, Graham, who hadn't accompanied us due to a "paddling" trip he already had planned (his new sport was kayaking), had returned home and decided to come and find us. He could see us from the banks of the loch and followed our slow progress with his binoculars, later teasing Jane about our less-than-direct course over the water. Time was getting on and in the end we had to put the engine on and motor the last leg into Gairlochy Top, to a lovely peaceful mooring pontoon, and with the water as flat as a mirror the mountain view was doubled by the reflection. Ducks were paddling their way around the water and the birds were singing in the early evening sunlight, and best of all, there was not a midge in sight! Graham arrived in time to join us for boat cocktails – a fairly limited choice, but none-the-less good ones – a choice of Gin & Tonic or Dark & Stormy (dark rum and ginger beer normally poured over ice with the rum floating on top of the ginger beer). Graham recommended a hotel back down the loch-side, where we could get a nice meal, and we headed off together in search of food in his new BMW5 sports, and it really felt like luxury travel after a week on board Grautvornix!

The lochside hotel had been there for many years, but it was clear that the dining room at least had undergone a major refurbishment, with dark stained solid wood tables and matching dining chairs and subtle décor. It's most appealing feature was the glorious view across the loch, and being such a beautiful evening, we were tempted to dine on the deck-like balcony, if it weren't for the threat of the dreaded wee beasties. We had a going-on with the waitress. You'd think that the owners of such an establishment, having gone to the trouble and expense of making the place look so sophisticated, would turn their attention to the staff. But, oh no. This lady was a feisty Scottish hen, who was only there as a favour to we customers. Why on earth should we expect polite, helpful service from her? The first thing that alerted us to this was her sucking-in of breath as she announced "Och I don't know if we can fit yous in the night". The four of us glanced round at the mostly empty tables. "So you're expecting a coach party any minute are you?" enquired Graham. Oh dear, I could feel the "grumpy old man" syndrome coming on! With enormous restraint, Graham proceeded to first chide, then tease, then coax the woman into submission. The change was remarkable – from being decidedly unhelpful during the seating and ordering process, to practically eating out of his hand and giggling like a schoolgirl by the time he'd finished with her. The meal came eventually and we mused over the situation whilst we ate. On the next table was an elderly couple who engaged Graham in conversation, or vice-versa if my memory serves me correctly. They were in their mid-to-late eighties and were absolutely charming. They were very smartly dressed, except he had his royal blue lambswool jumper on back-to-front, and were clearly enjoying their evening meal. We learned that they came to this same hotel every year and had done for the last 35 years. Not only that, they always drove up to Scotland from their hometown of Derby – nearly 400 miles!

Several beers later Jane (who doesn't like beer!) drove us back to the boat, amid much cheek from Graham about her driving, which was completely fine by the way. She was therefore less than delighted to hear that Graham had bought milk for the people on another boat, whom he had engaged in conversation whilst waiting for us. They had apparently asked Graham if there was anywhere to buy milk near Laggan Loch where they had moored-up, and were disappointed to find it was quite some distance to the nearest shop. Graham, wearing his "Mr Nice Guy" hat, had glibly offered to fetch it for them and deliver it back to them after our meal. We are now, you remember, in the Highlands, and the roads being what they are, it was quite some treck, and by now it was 10pm, but no matter. We reluctantly said our good-byes to our friends as they left us to make their milk delivery.

Back aboard Grautvornix we slept soundly and awoke to another lovely day and cast off the mooring ropes, headed for Gairlochy lock and swing bridge, bound for Banavie and Neptune's Staircase, a series of 8 locks. We went through the locks with several other boats, among them was "Miss Marple", a large motor-sailor that we had met earlier when they towed "the Lazyboys" into the safety of the canal from the tidal rips of the Moray Firth. It was a UK registered boat skippered by a Danish man who spoke excellent English, and his entire family plus friends and their families were all travelling together as one big happy crew. They had rigged a couple of children's swings up on the foredeck, hanging the down ropes to the boom. The children, some of them quite small, played confidently onboard, one of the smallest even taking her afternoon nap on deck under a mini quilt laid out for her. The skipper was a larger-than-life character, confidently in charge of the boat and her extended crew, and it seemed as though nothing would faze him – I could imagine their journey across the North Sea from Scandinavia had not worried him in the least. We travelled between the locks, as the gates opened to let us through, by taking the bow rope and the stern rope and "walking" the boat, which was fine for those with plenty of crew, however being only "2 up" I had the job of walking both ropes along the lockside wall, while Steve steered the boat from below. Not an easy task, especially when you're recovering from a broken wrist as I was. The sun was already high in the sky by now and the hot damp conditions of the canal brought out the midges – reach for the Deet!

There was another yacht in the lock from Denmark with a crew that were most definitely in holiday mode – during the time it took to fill-up the 8 locks and move us all through, they dressed two of the female crew in waitress outfits and sent them round the lockkeepers bearing trays of Schnapps! We must have had longing looks on our faces as very soon the tray was placed in front of us – the fiery liquid burned our throats but the after-glow was magic! Soon we were through all 8 of the locks and moored alongside the transit pontoons, awaiting a call from the lockkeeper of the Corpach

Basin, our next overnight stop. It was 2 hours before the basin was clear of boats coming through into the canal, so that we could take our place for the night prior to leaving the canal. We passed the time by going for a walk along the pretty canalside to stretch our legs and I picked wild flowers to adorn the boat's saloon – much to my skipper's disdain ("flowers on a boat?"). When the call came from the lockkeeper, we motored down to the Basin and brought Grautvornix alongside the wharf, secured the mooring lines and walked across to the village for provisions. Spotting a roadside pub we decided to pop in for a pint and a sandwich and escape the searing heat of the day (not often necessary in Scotland!). It was nice and cool inside – but that was about the best I could say of it. The business had obviously seen better days and was desperately in need of some TLC, the leather-look (plastic) seats were torn, the Formica (remember that?) tables were very old fashioned and the wallpaper was hanging off the wall in the corner. The elderly landlord had that startled look as we opened the door, as if he'd dozed off behind the bar and we had woken him. Still the sandwiches were fresh and the beer was cold – what more could we ask for?

We bought our provisions from the local Co-op store and made our way back to the boat. There were a couple of other boats in the basin by now, one of them "Stiefelchen" (Little Boot) and another large racing yacht with a crew of 8 young Scandinavian men, all exhorting and generally displaying the kind of macho behaviour that only young men can.

We later showered, changed and walked back along the canalside to the Lochy Bar for our evening meal – the pub was popular and full of boat owners and holiday makers in general, including the crew of "Miss Marple". Very full, very warm, and very red in the face (a combination of the food, beer and sunshine during the day) we made our way back along the waterside and fell happily into our double bunk in the forward peak.

Fort William to Oban

Saturday morning dawned and the sky once again was clear blue, the sun shining on the spectacular Scottish scenery and the wind virtually non-existent. We'd been at sea (or on canals) now for eight days and as the ninth day began we couldn't believe how lovely the weather had been – we had spent many holidays in Scotland over the years and had always described the weather as being very "Scottish" – that is to say, if you don't like it, wait five minutes! In fact I recall that the last time we were in this very village the rain had been torrential and the low clouds had almost hidden the view of Ben Nevis, which as we see this morning, stands majestically towering over us. It was hard to believe the shipping forecast, as we listened intently to the VHF at 7am that morning, when the announcer calmly said "Mull of Kintyre to Ardnamurchan Point: winds South Easterly gale force 8". I took comfort in the fact that our route today would take us down the length of Loch Linnhe, through the Lynne of Lorne to Oban, always in the shelter of the land.

Meanwhile, back in Scarborough the yacht club's annual North Sea Race had started. The texts began to arrive from our friends telling us there had been some bad weather in the days leading up to the race, resulting in a big swell, but the wind had died to nothing by Friday night and the start of the race had been a huge disappointment, with sails hanging loosely and boats wallowing about on the rolling sea. Our friend's boat Tomahawk reported taking an hour to get around the first mark, and by 10pm that evening was still in Filey Bay. Yacht Aeysha had already given up and put her engine on! Our commodore's boat Vado had made it out into the tide before the wind died completely and was in the lead, en route (albeit slowly) to Ijmuiden, Holland. Our thoughts were with them as we imagined the frustration of the long day and night ahead with very little wind to sail by.

Meanwhile we were out of the Corpach Basin and into Loch Linnhe, motor-sailing quite happily along and enjoying the scenery, sharing the loch with just a few small boats, passing Fort William to port and on to the Corran Ferry crossing point to Ardgour. I remember many times taking this ferry as we made our way in convoy with the diving club, on our annual diving trip to Lochaline in the Sound of Mull. There was always a tremendous feeling of excitement and anticipation as we reached the ferry, knowing we were on the last leg of our long journey to our favourite place of escape. I got that sensation of freedom that you feel when you're away from all of the responsibilities that one's day-to-day life carries.

To my delight a pod of porpoises were fishing in the loch, off Lismore Island, and the spectacle completed my picture of paradise!

Arrived Oban 13.15 hours – so stated the Log – and calling up the marina office we were directed to row A of the Kerrera pontoons. What a shock to the system – there were boats everywhere and the pontoons were all full with yachts rafted-up 3 or 4 abreast! We had joined the Classic Malts Cruise, along with over 100 other boats. Of course we weren't really surprised, we had heard about the Cruise and logged on to the website last winter. The idea appealed to us and, looking back, I'm really glad we did – it was such fun! We rafted-up alongside Kilrush, a boat crewed by four men who seemed friendly enough, and headed off to the office to pay for our overnight berth. The Cruise organisers had erected a marquee and there was a bar and a seafood barbeque – the smell was delicious – so we partook of a cold glass of white wine and bathed in the bonhomie and the sunshine. What a view lay in front of us – 110 boats laid out against the backdrop of the pretty town of Oban with the sun shimmering on the water in between. The Malts Cruise had laid on free water-taxis and soon we climbed aboard one, along with 63 other cruisers, which was slightly alarming considering the boat looked big enough for about half that number. Arriving safely, thank goodness, we disembarked onto Oban Pier and all headed to the Oban Distillery. There the Cruise organisers registered all arrivals and dished out flags, document bags, fleeces, crew shirts, caps and all manner of free logo-bearing gifts, so that all Cruise participants became immediately recognisable throughout the Western Isles! A walk through the town to buy boat supplies, then back on the crowded water-taxi, where we found ourselves in a squashed huddle with Roger & Gavin from Kilrush. It was only now we realised (the names should have been a clue) the predilection of the pair. We greeted each other in a friendly way and I turned to Roger to say something profound (I forget just what it was) only to find him gazing up at Steve in a very "girlish" way. Then it dawned on me – but Steve was oblivious and it wasn't until Gavin made a coarse retort to him (something about "taking it up the a**e like a man") that it dawned on him too. Now we're not homophobic or anything, but Steve suddenly felt distinctly uncomfortable with the crush on the boat!

The Classic Malts Cruise social event that evening was to be held in the Oban Distillery yard. There was a free buffet and a free bar all night – imagine the excitement! We made our way through the throng of people already assembled and collected our first drink (steady…) then did our favourite thing at these events: people-watching. To our surprise and delight, we found everyone wonderfully friendly and sociable and we met some very interesting people – there was Alison & Les from the yacht Islander of Menai, a very experienced crew who sailed professionally, but were part of the Cruise due to a cancelled booking. Alison, a pretty lady with dark hair, healthy-looking complexion and the bluest eyes I've ever seen, spoke with youthful enthusiasm about her love of sailing, while Les related the story of their sailing trip around the Falklands and how they sold one boat there to a local and flew back to the UK and bought another! They recommended sailing around Chile: "from Cape Horn following the coastline is quite stunning" they said. The Islander of Menai is a Soltram Saga 40, a beautiful yacht, and is available for charter, which is what they do now, and it transpired that a wealthy client had chartered it to sail from Amsterdam to the West coast of Scotland and join the Classic Malts Cruise. Unfortunately he had lost his passport in Italy and couldn't make it to Amsterdam in time, so they were instructed they should sail without him and he would catch them up in Oban. However, there was no sign of him as yet, so they were just doing the Cruise themselves, since it was all paid for in advance. Seemed good to me!

We met the Dutch skipper from a large sailing barge, and when we expressed our surprise at the number of boats joining the Cruise from all over Europe, he looked at us with that "isn't it obvious?" expression and said: "We are sailing around the best cruising ground in the whole of Europe!" He has a point. We also met the owners of the yacht Delinquent – a Dehler 34 – a pale couple, slightly eccentric-looking and their even-paler crew, a couple from Liverpool who looked as if they had been kept in a cupboard for the last year, only to be suddenly released out into the bright sunshine. It later transpired they had driven up to Oban to join the boat – straight from the cupboard, no doubt.

The wonderful buffet was a feast of seafood, meats & salads followed by fresh strawberries, cold sweets and a cheeseboard that would be the envy of any dinner table. The evening was completed by a full Scottish marching band and the sound was carried around the high stone walls of the Distillery yard, making me, and probably everyone else there that night, fervently wish they could claim Scottish ancestry!

Warmed by the Malts we'd tasted and basking in the late summer evening sun, we were all marched down to the quayside behind the band, feeling proud to be part of it all. And so to bed.

Back at the pontoons reality struck as the wind had increased dramatically (remember that gale force 8 they had talked about?) and the boats were being rocked about on their moorings. Some of the boats on the exposed ends of the pontoons were taking the swell and anchors were being dropped as a precaution. During the night the storm blew through and in the morning the sky was still cloud-laden and it was raining, which was a pity because a Parade of Sail had been organised, prior to the boats leaving. The parade went ahead, led by Spray of Wight, and all 110 boats struggled to get into a big circle following Spray and passing the pier, where a lone piper stood (looking a little soggy) to pipe us onwards. A bunch of brave onlookers stood next to the piper and waved from under their umbrellas. Most of the yachts managed to get into place, with a few stragglers bumbling about in the middle of the harbour, getting in the way of the Calmac ferry, which had to sound his five-blasts horn signal (which in nautical terms means "what the bloody hell are you doing?!") The Cruise organisers came over the VHF with the message:

"Thank you to all the boats taking part in the Classic Malts Cruise – see you all in Talisker – Yahoo!" Clearly too much malts-tasting the night before.

The long line of yachts left the harbour and headed out into the Sound of Mull, however, as exciting as the prospect was of making our way up to the Isle of Skye, we motored Grautvornix back to the pontoons and moored her up for one more night. We had been moving-on every day for the last 10 days and we felt like a day off. Besides, we didn't like sailing in convoy, and we knew all the other boats would be headed for Tobermory on Mull, where they would struggle for a berth, having once again to raft-up 3 or 4 abreast, so this way we could take our time and meander up to Mull later when it would be altogether more peaceful. We found an empty berth, paid our mooring fee, took our washing to the laundry (where you have to be a bit "pushy" this time of year as the machines are constantly in use) and headed off on the now-empty water taxi. We walked up to McCaig's Tower on the hillside above Oban and enjoyed the view. The sky had now cleared-out and the sun coming through again, and I read with interest the information about the tower's origins. I've visited the town many times before as part of our diving club's trip, but we always seemed to head straight for the Oban Inn, oddly enough, and I never took the time to explore the scenery properly. Funny that! I was dismayed to see that the Oban Inn has been closed and is now boarded up – the end of an era for us. Anyway, I digress, it seems the original Mr McCaig was a wealthy banker and property owner, who had the tower built partly as a memorial to his family, but also to give work to the many local stonemasons who were out of work during the long winter months. Now how strange is that – a rich man with a conscience!

Leaving the tower we headed off to the fish pier where we had been told we would find a crab stall belonging to the man who also owned the best seafood restaurant in the area. The Seafood Temple is situated on an elevated position above the bay and has the most stunning view of all the stunning views in Oban. Originally a toilet block, of all things, the owner has restored and refurbished it to a high standard and it is fitted-out with solid wooden tables and chairs, with a huge mirror along the back wall that reflects not only the light but the view as well. We were impressed with the setting, but when we got our meals we were truly in seafood-heaven. The scallop chowder that Steve chose was to die for, and the hot & cold smoked salmon with asparagus delicious. The main meals of scallops in creamy sauce were served in scallop shells on a huge silver tray, and were simply a work of art and I only wish that I had a bigger appetite so that I could have managed seconds! We took our coffee & malts outside sitting at the enormous solid pine table overlooking the bay and reflected on our good fortune – the restaurant is always fully booked but we had been very lucky as there was a cancellation that day. The owner came out to ask our opinions on the food, and told us he went to college in our hometown of Scarborough – small world. I texted our good friend Fred (author, diver & fishing magnate) and thanked him for the recommendation and we drank to absent friends.

Back in the real world, the washing wasn't dry, not enough money put in I suppose, and I had to relinquish the drier to the long queue of others wanting to use it. The result being damp washing hanging around the boat: "looks like a bloody Chinese laundry in here!" said Steve. We spent the rest of the evening discussing our plans for tomorrow, and the picturesque Tobermory was to be our next port of call.

Oban to Tobermory

It was Monday morning 08.15 hours and the glorious sunshine had already revealed itself to us. How much longer can this weather last? We motored out of the marina, put up the sails and headed across the Lynn of Lorne, past Lismore Lighthouse and on up the Sound of Mull under main and jib. The wind was picking up and, as we approached the Sound, there was Duart Castle standing proud on the headland with the islands and mountains fringing the panoramic view. By now there is a true-blue sky and wispy white clouds, with a bank of heavier cloud on the higher peaks; a midnight-blue sea with a short chop, and nothing around us but a small fish-farm vessel. Looking ahead up the Sound the fully-set sails of 6 or 7 yachts come into view, spread across the water they complete the perfect view, and Steve insists on adding to the atmosphere with his rendition of the Andy Stewart classic "I've just come down from the Isle of Skye".......

Two hours later and the wind had once again been reduced to "light airs" and we were ghosting up the Sound of Mull, making full use of the spinnaker, at a leisurely 3.5 knots. At Tobermory we are lucky to find a pontoon berth and moor-up Grautvornix with ease before heading off to check-out the new facilities building. It is a most impressive addition with good clean loos, showers, laundry and a visitors' centre. The next stop is MacGoggan's bar for a cool beer, where we sit and observe all the people and comings & goings of a tourist resort in full swing – there are people from all over the world here. When I first started coming to Tobermory there were very few tourists, it being a very long trek from most urban areas of the mainland. Only the hardy and the adventurous got this far in those days. I was very lucky to be taken there by Colin and his entourage – my early diving buddies. Colin had taken me under his wing as a newly qualified diver and he and his fellow boat-owners (they had their own RIB – which was something of a luxury back then) welcomed me into their circle of friends. We had the most amazing adventures as we explored the seabed around the west coast of Scotland. The fish and the crabs and lobsters were all there in their natural habitat, and finning slowly along, in and out of the seaweed beds, we had all the time in the world to watch them. Occasionally the seals would come and find us, curious about us and nibbling at our fins. We dived all the wrecks in the Sound of Mull and talked endlessly about what we'd seen: "I swam over the foredeck and along the companionway" and "did you see the moray eel in that broken pipe?" and "I went down into the engine room" and "there was a huge lobster under one of the collapsed plates on the stern".

Colin taught me how to "scallop" – and when we found the scallop beds they were so plentiful that we filled our "goody-bags" until we could barely drag them behind us! I had to inflate my buoyancy aid (an inflatable collar-like item that we wore over our drysuits) so that I could raise myself off the seabed when I was ready to surface. As soon as we were back on the boat, Colin would whip out his diving knife and deftly slit open one of the scallop shells, cutting out the flesh and feeding it to me raw – it was delicious!

"They don't come any fresher than that!" he would exclaim, and he was right. It saddens me now when we dive those beds and see the devastation caused by the scallop-dredgers that trawl huge nets along the seabed, destroying everything in its path, leaving bare-naked sand in its wake. It will take years for those beds to recover.

Back at our base in Lochaline we cooked the scallops in white wine and had a feast fit for royalty. Of course divers nowadays know Lochaline as a popular base as it now boasts a Dive Centre with all modern facilities, but when we first went there it was a tiny village with nothing but the odd B&B. A friend of Colin kept an old caravan on the quayside along with a battered old Land Rover that just about got him around. We pitched our tents on the grass by the side of these and we cooked "al-fresco" on a makeshift cooker set-up on the bonnet of the Land Rover. It didn't rain at all during that first diving trip to Lochaline and Tobermory, unusual for Scotland even though it was July, and I have the most wonderful memories of Blue Star – that was the name of the RIB – powering up the Sound of Mull in the sunshine, with a blue sky and the beautiful Highland scenery for a backdrop. I felt like the luckiest person in the world.

"We will need provisions for the next couple of days, since we have decided to take a detour up Loch Sunart" I said to Steve. We had heard that it is stunning but isolated. So off we go to Tobermory's main street, where we are surprised to see that the old church, once converted into a local crafts centre, is now a Spar Shop! With our victuals bought and stowed, we hang around the boat for a bit, enjoying the peace and the scenery, and indulging in a "yachty's" favourite pastime: people & boat watching.

The most famous pub in Tobermory is the Mishnish – it's been there for years and is full of history and local atmosphere. It has been modernised, albeit in quite an appropriate style, but now somehow it just doesn't feel the same. The owner's yacht is moored opposite the pub, with a banner advertising the Mishnish, and we watched him as he served his customers, "like a loaded gun, about to go off at any moment" observed Steve (he had rubbed Steve up the wrong way immediately). I also felt a bit intimidated by his presence, and by the atmosphere of the pub generally, which was a shame because we had known this place for many years as our favourite watering-hole after diving. The pub had been owned by a local accordionist, Bobby McLeod, and I believe it may still be in the family. A lot has changed on Tobermory waterfront, some of the changes down to the filming of the popular children's TV programme Balamory. The crew of Miss Marple arrived and settled-into a corner table. On leaving, we bump into their friends from the yacht Antalis, and we direct them to the Mishnish to join them.

Back at home, we have a print of a painting by Hamish McDonald of the fishing pier, looking towards the clock tower and we now stand beneath the tower and discover that a local lady, in memory of her sister who died of dysentery, commissioned it. I love that painting because it depicts a different view of the town, instead of the usual row of colourful buildings facing the harbour, which is also lovely but can be seen too often. Later we make the most of the long daylight hours and the fine weather by eating outside at McGoggan's – fish pie seemed appropriate for this setting around the harbour. We stroll back to the boat and observe the occupants of the boat moored next to ours, who have 3 children with them aged from around 18 months to 6 years, and we marvel that people can achieve both a sailing holiday and look after such young children at the same time! The children are remarkably well behaved.

Later I listened to Radio 4 and heard the sad news of the deaths of 9 British soldiers in Afghanistan. I have mixed feelings – on the one hand I hate war and the terrible waste of human life that it entails, whilst on the other hand I abhor terrorism and the use of mass violence to enforce an ideal. There has to be an answer in negotiation – surely we have reached a point in civilisation where we can sit around a table and talk through our differences?

I go to bed with a very heavy heart and we are both awoken by the sound of a heavy storm in the night, we hear the Tobermory clock strike 3am. I hear it chime

4am as I lie awake with Steve sleeping soundly, I switch on my torch and try to read. Apparently there were otters on the pontoon during the night – how I wish I had got up instead of trying to read by torchlight!

We awoke to a lovely clear morning and blue sky, with very little wind, and carried out Steve's plan – to photograph Grautvornix in the harbour with the town as the backdrop, and send a copy to various friends back in Scarborough (echoes of our Windrift trip 4 years ago). This involved leaving the pontoon mooring, taking fenders in, blowing-up the rubber dinghy, picking-up and tying to a mooring buoy in the middle of the harbour, paddling the dinghy out to a suitable point (with 2 cameras round neck) taking at least a dozen photos from all angles (and waiting for clouds to move across sun), paddling back to boat, getting dinghy on board, slipping ropes off mooring buoy, tying fenders on, returning to pontoon (someone already in our place!) finding a vacant space, swapping fenders from port to starboard side, mooring up to pontoon. Then walking to the local chemist shop, viewing prints on printing machine (very state-of-the-art for a small town island chemist!) and selecting the best, before printing 10 copies to send with a message on the reverse. Steve already had pre-printed envelopes (very organised) and this left just a visit to the post office for stamps and posting – phew! Mission accomplished. Now perhaps we can get on with the trip!

Isle of Mull to Isle of Skye

We finally left Tobermory at 11am and hoisted the main and the jib – there was very little wind and we crossed the Sound of Mull under motor-sail and entered Loch Sunart. Alternating between sailing and motor-sailing, as the wind came and went, with clouds gathering all around us, we looked back to see black storm clouds over Tobermory. Our way up the Loch was as calm as could be, with water like oil beneath the hull, the GPS plotter kept us on the right track, avoiding the shallows and any hidden pinnacles. Once again we marvelled at the peace and tranquillity of the whole area, and tried to appreciate fully just how beautiful this part of Scotland really is. As we approached Saleen Bay, right at the head of the Loch, the keeper came out to meet us in his small dinghy and guided us to the visitors' moorings. We were given details of the facilities and told where the nearest shop and pub were. He took our mooring fee of £15 and when we asked about a water taxi to shore, he told us it would be £6 each way. We decided to use our own dinghy, which unfortunately had sprung a small leak, however being tight Yorkshire folk, at the thought of saving £12 we decided we would manage. The plan was to paddle ashore, take a walk through the local countryside, pick-up some provisions, have a meal in the pub and paddle back to the boat for an early night. That didn't quite work out. We inflated the dinghy and set off ashore with Steve manfully handling our one paddle from side to side, with me perched behind. Pretty soon I noticed water swilling about in the bottom around my feet – I had on my wellies, so no matter. Then I noticed the water was now over my feet and washing the bottom of my trousers, no sooner had I called to Steve to "paddle faster!" than I felt the cold water against my skin! Seated low-down as I was, the water had seeped through both layers of my clothing: "Hurry! We're sinking!" was my next cry. There was nothing I could do – Steve was paddling furiously and bathed in sweat from the exertion, and all I could do was sit tight and hope we made it to shore. We pulled the dinghy alongside the pier and climbed out, our clothes sodden and the dinghy a limp heap of rubber on the slipway. We took off our wet-weather gear and spread it out on the wall to dry and walked up the hill, squelching all the way, to the pub where we ordered a couple of beers to cheer us up. What to do now? We couldn't go for a long walk as planned as our footwear was soaking, as were our trousers, and we weren't even sure the dinghy would make it back to the boat. We might have to swim! There was no choice but to try and make it back and we would spend the evening on board. Back at the jetty, we gathered our gear and inspected the forlorn-looking tender. Just then the pier-man arrived and started to climb into his dinghy, which, joy of joys, had an outboard motor! "Any chance of a tow, mate?" Steve enquired. He looked at us for a moment, then said "Ok – pass me your painter" and we rather gingerly climbed back into the limp dinghy. His little motor struggled with the weight of the tow, but we set off towards the middle of the Loch where Grautvornix was moored. We moved much more quickly this time, but unfortunately the leak was worse, and the water coming in even faster – I wished I had thought to find a bailing bucket! We were soaked again in no time – I thought of the ignominy of us slowly sinking under the water and having to swim the last few yards. By the time we came alongside Grautvornix we were knee-deep in water, but miraculously still afloat (almost!). We climbed out of the water onto the ladder and dragged the deflated rubber thing that had been our tender onto the boat. Hanging our wet gear on the guard rails Steve busied himself with jobs about the boat, and there are always plenty of those: renewing the elastics on the barber haulers, re-fuelling the stove igniters etc. and we resigned ourselves to a long afternoon and evening aboard. I stripped the bedding off the bunk and draped it over the boom to air and then made us a late lunch and settled myself on deck to admire the view. The water was so clear I felt like a swim – but I didn't bring my costume. At the other side of the loch a pair of herons was patiently waiting for fish; the oyster-catchers could be heard calling to each other across the water. I watched as another couple of boat-owners prepared to load-up their yacht for a passage. They spent an age loading the small tender (they had an outboard motor on theirs – lucky things!)

then transporting everything across to the boat in three separate trips. It seemed a sleepy little place, but I bet there were eyes everywhere! Later that evening I cooked us a very tasty hot pasta dish – amazing what you can do on a small stove – and when we could no longer read our books (nodding-head syndrome) we went to bed and slept soundly.

At 05.00 hours we silently slipped the mooring and motored gently out of Salen Bay and along the silent shores of Sunart. There was no wind at all and the loch was like a mirror. The light wasn't black & white, but various shades of grey. The couple that loaded their boat the night before, still had not left. As our bow slowly and silently parted the water, a shoal of flying fish flew out of the water, their bellies shining in the sunlight. Two hours later we were within sight of our exit from the loch and to my delight three porpoises surfaced out of the water and swam along with us. We reached the Sound of Mull and shifted our course towards Arisaig. The weather had changed and the sky had become dramatic with every shade of grey to black, then came the rain, and heavy, like it does in Scotland. Calmac ferries were visible in all directions, and with the sea still very flat, we spotted several seals popping their heads up and looking around at us. A large dolphin arched above the surface several times and the guillemots were massing all around us, only bobbing under the water as we approached. They seemed to enjoy a game of "who dares wait until the boat is upon us?!" I went below and made bacon sandwiches for Steve and a bowl of muesli for me, followed by several cups of hot coffee to keep us going through the rain.

Passing the Point of Ardnamurchan I commented on how lucky we were to have this weather, as we had heard many tales of hair-raising experiences by others sailing around this point in heavy seas. Later I telephoned Arisaig marina – and was told they had no water taxis available and they were not sure there was a berth for us, but promised to ring back when other boats decided to leave – they didn't though. We later decided to head on to Armadale on the SE side of Skye. What a journey – the scenery is amazing! We could see all the islands of the Inner Hebrides – Muck, Rum, Eigg, and in the distance the Outer Hebrides and the Little Minch in between. Armadale lies opposite the mainland town of Mallaig – much bigger than I had imagined – and the scene of activity over on the coast fascinated me, as I watched through the boat's binoculars. The Calmac ferry was making it's way towards the terminal at the pier in Armadale Bay and we though it wise to hang back until it had entered the bay – never argue with a Calmac ferry! The moorings were easy – a boat came out to guide us to ours and offered information about the local services, where to get water & diesel etc. They kindly gave us a ride to the shore and arranged a return trip at 5pm.

After taking advantage of the shower facilities, we strolled through the sunny lanes to the local pub and enjoyed a pint in the sunshine, chatting to some tourists that were also making the most of the weather. On the way to the local shop, we passed a carthorse being led to where an antique carriage was waiting. The view across to the Scottish mainland was dramatic and rugged and the mountains were constantly changing with the light. We tried to buy a 2nd hand tender, without any luck, from the local boatyard that was a treasure-trove of boat paraphernalia. We bought provisions from the local shop that cost almost as much as a week's shopping in Tesco, and made our way back to the marina, where our lift was waiting. After cooking a meal and enjoying a glass of wine in the evening air, we planned tomorrow's route and programmed the GPS. I spent a restless night, and finally gave up on sleep, moving back into the saloon to read, rather than disturb Steve. I didn't bother with the torch this time!

We left Armadale early, after the first ferry had docked. There was more wind today and we motor-sailed to the Point of Sleat, when we were able to knock the engine off and sail with main & jib. Just before that, as we reached the point, there was a strange noise from the engine – or was it the prop? – and I felt a vibration on the tiller. The wind had died to nothing and as I took the revs off for Steve to investigate, the sea had an uncomfortable motion. I looked around and saw the rocks of the point were dangerously close as we wallowed helplessly for a few moments, and my stomach muscles tightened as I quickly assessed the potential situation – what if the engine failed? There was no wind to manoeuvre us out of danger! Steve's head appeared from the engine box, I gave him an expectant look and he said "can't see anything wrong down there – set her on again". With relief I put some revs on and steered her away from the coastline. We decided it must have been some underwater obstruction that had caught us. The wind soon came back and as we sailed in sight of the Isle of Skye coastline, we marvelled at the beautiful scenery across the water – the islands of first Muck then Eigg – flat-topped like Table Mountain – then Rum with it's many peaks and fascinating cloud formation above, like an icing-topping. The western coastline of Skye is very dramatic, much of it inhospitable cliffs & rock right down to the shoreline – no beaches on this bit! The only vegetation seemed to be grass with no trees visible at all, unlike the coastline we had just left on the east side which had woodland plantations. Several fishing boats were active in the area and there was a smattering of yachts in sight in the distance – were they some of our "Classic Malts" people?

The news came on the radio and we listened to the report of the homecoming of the bodies of 8 British soldiers, killed in action in Afghanistan. People lined the streets to pay tribute as the coffins filed by, and I thought: "The world keeps turning; life goes on. But not for the mothers of those boys."

At 15.00 hrs we arrive at Loch Harport – the bay alive with yachts of all sizes anchored in neatly arranged rows. The large white-painted building directly in front of them all immediately identifiable with TALISKER painted on in huge black letters. Looking at the depth gauge we notice that the water in the bay is pretty deep and wonder if the anchor chain is long enough! To our relief, a large RIB zooms over to greet us and directs us to a spot close in-shore where the depth gauge shows us we have 10m of water below the boat. Dropping the anchor and relaxing into the moment, I look around at the magnificent view. It is a lovely sheltered loch with superb scenery all around and a small clutch of single-storey houses in the distance. Water-taxis were provided by the Classic Malts organisers and no sooner had we called-up on channel 72 than one arrived to take us ashore. Great service!

There was evening entertainment planned for us all, in the form of a hot buffet meal followed by a Ceilidh, so we were keen to attend to all the necessary provisioning etc. before joining the rest of the crews at 7pm. Walking past the distillery and up the hill to the local shop (one and only!) we were surprised to find it packed to the door – mostly with Germans! One of them had very thoughtlessly taken his can of diesel into the shop, so that the whole place stank of fuel-oil. The shop owners were hurriedly packing shopping into bags for the growing number of customers, with huge smiles on their faces – I bet they had never had this many people in the shop before. It was another hot sunny day and they were doing a roaring trade in iced lollies. We really needed bags of ice to cool our milk etc. not having a fridge on board, but no luck. We bought a bag of frozen peas instead – Steve insisted that would do the trick – and we marched back down the hill, stopping only to buy several bottles of Talisker whisky to take home for our friends. The water taxi was there to ferry us back to Grautvornix and we relaxed on deck with a cold beer each and talked over our plans for the next day. We had been speaking to the skipper of Kilrush, our new friends whom we met in Oban, who had told us of their sightings of a shoal of 30 basking sharks and some minke whales in the Sound of Canna. So excited were we at this, that we changed our plans and decided to sail on the early tide the following morning, straight across to Canna, in the hope of seeing these amazing creatures. We have first-hand experience of how enormous they are, having once been in the water with basking sharks off the isle of Tiree, some years ago, when we were on a diving trip. They are awesome – in the true sense of the word (not the modern sense as in simply meaning "good"). However, this new plan involved getting up at some un-earthly hour to ensure the tide was on our side – which we are indeed used to doing – but probably not after a night on the Talisker! We jointly resolved not to over-do the drinking.

The evening sky was still brilliant-blue with white fluffy clouds and the sun bright enough for sunglasses, as we hailed a water-taxi and joined the people gathering outside the huge marquee, erected for the event. People milled around chatting and sipping their drinks, enjoying the warmth of a summer evening and the rarity of being able to socialise in the open-air in Scotland in the evening! The organisers had done a splendid job – everything was provided to make the evening a success, including the most popular item: the anti-midge spray. There was a bottle on every surface outside and people were making the most of it. It was after all perfect midge conditions, being right by the water's edge. The evening was great! We all enjoyed a very tasty supper – hot beef & vegetables, or in my case a vegetarian alternative, followed by a selection of sweets & cheeses, then the band struck-up and the Ceilidh began. The musicians were all local Scots and they had the floor full of dancers almost on the first note! Everyone was in the mood for dancing – and soon had created an atmosphere of real jollity and fun. We met up with our friends from Islander of Menai and shared several sailing tales together. Les & Alison introduced us to another couple – Murray & Margaret – who were a great hoot! Murray was a "proper" Scot – he had the accent, the kilt and the tales to go with it! He taught us all about the Scottish traditions, and even talked us through the quite complicated traditional sequence-dance that was being enacted on the dance floor. Steve was by now trying to persuade me to leave, he having been sensibly drinking, however I, on the other hand, had not. Oh he's such a party-pooper! I'm fine. I'll just have one more…..

In the end he got cross and threatened to leave without me – his sensible head telling him that the crossing tomorrow would not be a smooth one. I reluctantly agreed to go (but I was having such a good time!) and followed him down to the waiting water taxi.

At 04.30hrs the next morning I wished I'd listened to Steve. We "readied" the boat, pulled-up the anchor and silently slipped out of the bay and on down Loch Harport towards the open sea. The wind had freshened and a big swell was running, making the crossing uncomfortable, with the wind directly behind us it was difficult to set the sails, and as conditions worsened I began to get worried. This had not been forecast! We had started off with the full main and the Jib, but now we had to reduce the sail area. I took the helm while Steve went to the mast to put a reef in the main. By the time he had done that and come back to the cockpit, the wind was blowing even stronger – we could hardly hear each other over the noise of the wind &

waves, and the sails kept flapping madly and the boom threatened to jibe across as the boat was thrown about in the swell. The Jib would have to come down, but I hated the idea of Steve going up to the bow in these conditions. It had to be done, and I must take the helm again, which by now I was having difficulty holding, so tight was the pressure on the rudder. I watched terrified as Steve battled against the wind and tried to keep control of the madly-flapping sail that wanted to fly off into the ocean! He managed it, and dragged it back to the cockpit, afraid of tying it to the guard-rail in case the storm took it, and he quickly stowed it below. I shouted to Steve "we've still got too much sail area – we could be knocked down!" "Shall I get the storm Jib and take the main down?" Steve shouted back. "Just get rid of the main!" I cried as the swell took the boat up to the top of a massive wave. Steve decided this was too much – it would be almost impossible in these conditions – and although I was desperate to get rid of the cause of the boom thrashing threateningly, I also realised how risky it was sending Steve back to the mast. What a dilemma! "We'll wait 'till we get through the Straits and behind the island – should be some shelter there to sort this out!" yelled Steve above the din. Easier said than done, as we rose on each swell and surfed madly down the other side.

It is true that the island of Rum is a huge lump rising dramatically out of the sea, and in theory should have a lee side – but what actually happens is that the wind funnels round from both sides and meets in the middle at the so-called Leeward side! We tucked-in as close as we dare to get what little shelter there was, and I held on tightly to the helm while Steve fought his way to the mast and struggled heroically to get the mainsail down. This seemed to take forever (I'm sure it wasn't really that long but it's amazing how time slows down in a crisis situation) and my heart was thumping as I fought to keep the boat into the wind, in order to give Steve some slack. My worst fear at that moment was the nearness of the island rocks, and the thought of being blown ever closer before we could get control again. Suddenly it was down!

So this is where we came in – many pages ago – and the rest of the trip is the homeward leg that was to take quite a bit longer than the outward journey.

Rounding Ardnamurchan Point we reflected on the vast difference in the conditions between our Skye-bound outward passage and this one – a flat sea afloat with guillemots had been replaced by 3m high rolling swells and thrashing winds. I remembered how we'd actually had our breakfast on deck – whereas now, though both starving hungry as we hadn't eaten since last night, there was no chance of the merest nibble of a biscuit. We could not have contemplated going below, where everything had been thrown into mayhem with the violent movement of the boat. For the same reason we dare not take a drink of water – the thought of having to go below, remove our clothing, and try to use the heads was inconceivable! Apart from not being able to keep upright long enough to accomplish this normal everyday task, I knew if I ventured below I would be sea-sick – and that was the last thing we needed. I thought then of a past experience of severe sea-sickness, when I had become completely incapacitated as a result, thereby causing my fellow crew much annoyance & inconvenience. I'll take a short break from this story and tell you about it.

Steve & I were crewing for some friends of ours who were delivering a 60ft yacht, Shaman, from the Dominican Republic to Bermuda (nice job if you can get it!). Flying into Dominican we were met by Jon & Tracy who drove us down to the marina. It was a brand new marina, not yet completed, and we boarded Shaman in great excitement. Then came the rain. I've never seen rain like it! Everything was flooded in minutes and it was just like a curtain – you could barely see through it! After stowing our gear we familiarised ourselves with the yacht and were given the necessary safety information, were introduced to the other members of the crew, and we all headed off to a local beach bar. Normally everyone would sit outside and the barbeque would be lit, but on this occasion we stayed inside due to the weather and got to know each other over a beer. The next morning our passage would begin. We were up bright and early with the sun – yes the sun was shining and in no time at all it was hot and humid – the rain from the day before had evaporated and we at least caught a glimpse of how the Dominican normally looks, before we cast off the ropes and motored out of the marina and away on our journey. The first 3 days sailing were "a doddle". The sun shone, the sea was flat and the wind light. The boat practically sailed herself; she had all-electric winches for hoisting and adjusting the sails. The mainsail stored itself into the boom and the headsail was self furling. Everything on board was controlled by computer: the ballast tanks, the water tanks, the fuel tanks and the engine all were monitored and displayed on computer screen. Even the stereo system was computerised. There was a complete library of books, videos and DVDs on board. During the day we streamed fishing lines from the stern and caught beautifully fresh fish for dinner. Our watch-system allowed for some "down time" when we were free to take advantage of the boat's goodies.

We crossed the Sargasso Sea and headed into the wide-open North Atlantic where our wonderful sail turned into a much wilder affair. We were on watches, 2 hours on the helm, 2 hours on boat-duty, and 2 hours sleep, which worked very well until I was struck down. The actual act of being sick didn't bother me at all, I'd got used to coping with it during diving expeditions when I threw-up between kitting-up and couldn't wait to get under the water where all would become calm again. No, it was the blinding head-ache that went with it that did for me (as they say) I tried desperately to get rid of the pain with tablets and plenty of water, but every time I threw-up they went for a burton! This happened over and over until finally, when I was awoken for my watch, I simply could not raise my head from the pillow because of the knife that was being stabbed repeatedly into the top of my skull. Whilst wedged into my bunk with the lee cloth tightly fastened, the pain was just about manageable, but if I moved the merest fraction, the knife came down again into my head. At that point I gave in. To my enduring shame, I left my fellow crew to do a double-watch whilst I lay miserably a-bed. As soon as we neared Bermuda the weather improved, and so did my condition, and I was back on duty trying extra hard to pull my weight.

So back on Grautvornix I determined not to risk any such scenario. We fought manfully (and womanfully!) on until we reached the safety of the Sound of Mull and it was with huge relief that we motored into Tobermory Bay. So happy were we to have made it, that we celebrated with a couple of fried egg sandwiches. Also moored-up on the pontoons was Miss Marple – their skipper told us they hadn't made it to Skye due to generator problems, as he said this he was eyeing our Talisker flag that was fluttering on the halyard – "oh I didn't get one of those!" he exclaimed, and I think that hurt him more than the fact that the boat had been out of action!

The showers that night felt wonderful as I washed away the salt and the stress of the day. The rest of the "recovery treatment" consisted of a couple of beers and fish & chips on the pier watching the evening sky.

Return to the Caledonian

It was Saturday 18th July 2009 and we had been at sea for a whole 15 days, about half of our planned timescale. Already it was time to move on again and at 09.15hrs we slipped the ropes and motored across the bay, heading back into the Sound of Mull en-route to Dunstaffnage Marina. The previous night had not been good and the swell from the strong winds that developed had kept me awake most of the night. So bad was the rocking of the boat, that I woke Steve and asked him to go out and check the mooring ropes. He assured me that he had put down extra ropes before going to bed, and promptly went back to sleep. I must have eventually dropped off and when I awoke at 7am I had the strangest sensation that the boat was no longer floating on water – there was absolutely no movement. I went on deck to check what had happened and found the harbour as calm as a lake with no sign of the wind that had been so strong in the night.

Down the Sound there were lots of yachts out and the usual Calmac ferries running back & forth. The forecast was NW 3 to 4 going 5 to 6 later but we got

Arriving Caledonian Canal

Russ, Alana & Steve – finally get their photograph

Grautvornix on the waiting pontoons

A tranquil day on Loch Ness

Kerrera moorings – about to register for the Classic Malts Cruise

Truly a Seafood Temple, Oban

Grautvornix in Tobermory Bay

Loch Harport, Skye

Talisker Distillery on Skye

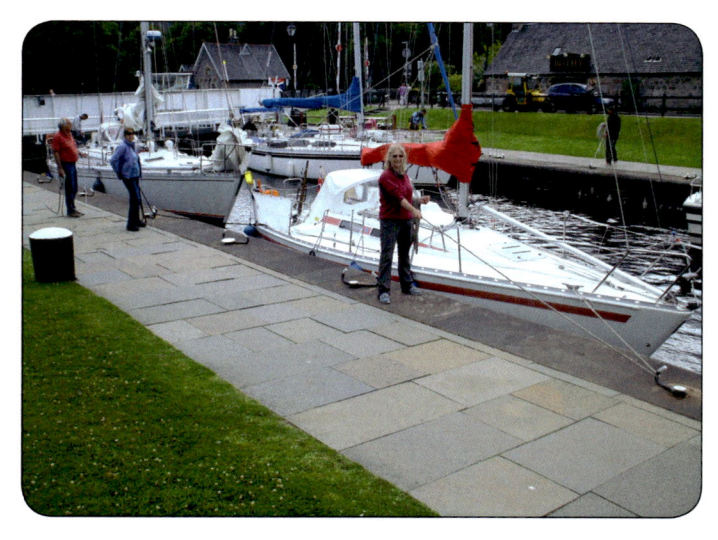

Locks on the Caledonian Canal

Clachnaharry Lock, Caledonian Canal

Our naval escort leaving the Sea Lock

Steve enjoys the evening sun in Lossiemouth

White-knuckle ride to Whitehills

Stonehaven looking deceptively calm

End of the journey – Scarborough in sight

force 3, which would have made it a very pleasant sail indeed. The wind however was directly behind us and we managed a very slow pace, finally giving-in and putting the engine on to motor-sail with the jib only. The sky was full of cloud – a mixture of grey & fluffy to quite black over the heights in the distance. A little rain was falling but it didn't dampen our spirits. Passing Lochaline I got a text from one of my diving buddies, Anne, telling me that she and her diving party had got the steering binnacle they had been after from a wreck in the Orkneys! This was great news as I knew they would be bringing this prize find to the diving club for display, alongside all the other precious artefacts that our diving members had recovered over the years. For those reading this who know something about wreck-finds, can I just reassure you that all our club's artefacts have been disclosed to the Receiver of Wrecks!

I got on the VHF and radioed-up the Dunstaffnage Marina and was allocated a pontoon berth – Echo 8 to be precise – but by the time we entered the harbour mouth, the wind had increased substantially and the rain was now beating down, hampering the visibility, and to make matters worse there was someone already on berth E8. I called-up the marina office once more and was given an alternative berth – Alpha 5 – and we brought the boat around, managing not to get blown off course, and not to hit anything! After tying-up securely to the pontoon cleats, we took a look at our surroundings and found the 150-berth marina to be very nice, with good facilities – a shop & chandlery, a laundry room and a great new shower/toilet block. After speaking to the marina manager, (who incidentally also runs the shop and we had to wait for him to finish his display and take several VHF calls!) we headed for the pub/restaurant where we booked a table for later that evening. Walking on into the village along the main road, we were astounded at the amount of traffic, and more than that, at the noise! After being at sea for over 2 weeks we had got used to the sound of nature, which is a very different kind of sound. And this was very hard on our ears! Later, after taking our washing to the laundry room, we went back to the restaurant for dinner. It happens that the restaurant was serving a special 3-course buffet that evening, and had laid-on a piper who played the bagpipes on the lawn in front of the dining room, with the marina as a backdrop, which was delightful. The food was good and the owners were obviously working hard at making the business successful (we thought they were eating in the restaurant themselves, as a very smartly-dressed couple were receiving extra service & attention!) and they had also booked a guitar duo who entertained with some wonderful music and singing. We did our usual people-watching and were intrigued by a party of French sailors who had sailed over from Nantes. There were other couples, who had clearly come for the food and had travelled there by car rather than boat, and these were distinguished by their "troughing". This is an expression Steve & I use to describe those among us who take particular delight in the "all you can eat" restaurants, and proceed to demolish trough-loads of food in the blink of an eye. Suddenly the place seemed appropriately named – The Wide Mouthed Frog!

Meanwhile the rain outside was lashing down, and we donned our weatherproof coats and headed back to the boat. On the way I called in at the laundry room to switch the wet clothes from the washer to the drier and had a bit of a "going on" as we say in Yorkshire. Whether it was the red wine or the lateness of the hour I don't know, but I miss-read the instructions and put the wet clothes into the drier and pressed the button for the washer/drier next to it with someone else's clean, and more importantly dry, clothes in it. When I heard the rush of water I knew there was something wrong. I quickly left the building!

On Sunday morning we were on our way up the Lynn of Morven and heading for Loch Linnhe by 10am, the wind was SE 2/3 and all behind us, and once again we had to motor-sail with just the Jib. All around us the sky was constantly changing, there were some blue patches but on the whole it was mostly grey with some black clouds hanging low over the highland peaks. Being out at sea one can watch the weather coming across the water and we could see patches of heavy rain making their way towards us until we were in the middle of a torrential downpour. We had the tide with us so we made quite good speed, arriving at Corpach Sea Lock at 1400hrs. There is a double lock and a road/rail bridge to go through/under and we were waiting for the go-ahead with 3 other boats: Joker, Islander & Lorna Mohr. The lock-keepers of the Caledonian Canal are a good bunch of guys and for the most part really friendly and helpful. It seems that from time-to-time their patience is tested, and so it was this day. The crew of the yacht Joker had called-up on the VHF from further down Loch Linnhe to ask the lock-keeper, no actually to TELL the lock-keeper, that they needed to be taken up Neptune's Staircase today. When told that could not be guaranteed, due to the number of boats waiting to go up, and the working-time constraints, the caller asked rather curtly "well what time are you working till?"! Rude I call it. The keepers must also see some cases of sheer incompetence too, as we did that day, and as a result we got very worried in the first lock as the water surged in, bouncing the yachts about as it does, and the bow of the boat at the other side of the lock came careering across the water as they let the ropes that secured them to the canal-side go. The keeper's quick action in throwing them a mooring rope saved us all from a collision. Whilst we were waiting to go into the first lock, the skipper from Lorna Mohr amused us by yelling military-style to his crew of two, who, it turned out later, consisted of a middle-aged man who had some sailing experience and a middle aged woman who had none. The poor lady had failed to throw the mooring rope to the lock keeper correctly, and it landed with a splash in the canal. When that happens it is very stressful as everyone else in the lock is watching, along with all the tourists lined-up on the canal-side, and you have to haul the dripping rope back on-board, coil it and throw it again. All the while the boat is drifting away from the canal wall and towards the boat at the other side. Anyway, the skipper decided that rope-throwing lessons were in order and in a very loud voice, yelled instructions to his hapless crew, while they practiced the throwing technique. Later whilst "walking" the boat up the canal (I was by now quite an expert at this!) I learnt that the skipper was a climber and operated two specialist climbing shops in

Sheffield. This accounted for his military-style modus operandum, which he clearly required during difficult and/or dangerous climbing trips. It was his plan to take the boat across the North Sea to the Kiel Canal and the Baltic Sea. He was using a team of friends to crew the boat in stages, with his wife flying out to join him later in Norway.

When we were through the last lock of Neptune's Staircase, Steve disappeared below and came back with several tot glasses of Talisker malt whisky which he distributed among the lock-keepers to show our appreciation of their patience and helpfulness. Needless to say this went down well! While we were passing the boats through the locks there were many tourists who enjoyed watching the spectacle and one lady shouted down to Steve from the canal-side "I think you're very brave – I get scared if there's too much water in the bath!"

Later we walked along the canal side to the Lochy pub, where we had eaten on the outward trip, and found it once again popular with tourists. We sat at the table next to a family group consisting of German grandma and father (Omar und Vater as the Germans would say), a Spanish mother and a bi-lingual daughter aged around 4 years. I was fascinated to hear such a little girl operating on such a linguistic level as she swapped effortlessly between the two languages.

During the night there were heavy showers on and off, and they continued throughout the next morning. We left our mooring at 08.00hrs and passed through Gairlochy into Loch Lochy (love that name!), on to Laggan Swing Bridge, Laggan Lock and out into Loch

Oich (another good name). Arriving in Fort Augustus we found the usual gridlock – this time there were 3 naval vessels, 2 large barges plus the usual yachts and motor cruisers. The naval boats: Explorer, Raider & Example, were taking navy cadets on a training exercise and were most impressive. Because of the number of vessels, we didn't get through the five locks and into the basin below until almost 18.00hrs. We had made contact with our friends Graham & Jane, who were entertaining their two nieces and a nephew, and we rushed off to the Bothy where they were already tucking-in to dinner. The children were all hungry after a hectic day with Auntie & Uncle. It was great to see them all together, and the children all had pink faces from the warm atmosphere and the excitement of the night-out.

Listening to the radio later, back on the boat, we learned that a fishing boat had gone down at Ardnamurchan Point that day with the loss of three lives. I looked over at Steve and we both remembered that very point, only three days ago, when we had fought to control our boat in the storm, and a cold shiver went down my spine.

It's Thursday 21st July 2009 and we're back on Loch Ness, this time recording a depth of 224 meters! We're motoring, because once again the wind is on the nose and at force 1 there is not much we can do about it. But the sky is blue and the sun is shining, making a great photo opportunity. Passing Urquhart Castle we are close enough to see all the tourists crawling around the grounds and, in the distance, all the tourist coaches that bring them on the "Lochs & Glens" tours. How glad we are to be here on the water with no-one to disturb us and the best view of the castle by far! Part of their tour will no doubt take them to the Clansman Hotel where, as we pass, we can see a huge purple plastic model of Nessie – "one to miss" as Steve would say! There is a small commercial marina there too, with motor-boats tied-up ready to take the tourists around the loch – one approaches us and abruptly turns through 180 degrees to enable the people on board to take photos of a yacht on the loch (ours!) and we pass close enough for us to see they are mostly Japanese tourists. We also pass some beautiful gardens which, on checking the chart, I discover are called Abriachan Gardens and I make a note to visit them next time we're in the area.

Into Dochgarroch Lock and through to the Tomnahurich swing bridge, we decide to tie-up to the waiting-pontoons as the bridge-keeper is having his lunch break. I quickly put some lunch together for us and we sit on deck to watch the world go by, watching mostly the commercial boat operators coming & going with their passengers on board – "Sail the Loch – Live the Dream!" proclaims the advertising board. Mini coaches wait to ferry the passengers back into Inverness – God forbid that they should have to walk anywhere! Passing through as the swing bridge is opened, we watch hoards of fat tourists in shorts video the canal and its traffic, and laugh to see those doing the filming being filmed themselves by other video-makers. I wonder how many of their friends back home will be "entertained" by these shots.

When we reach Muirtown Flight we are told we cannot pass though as the three naval training vessels are to be taken down the locks first; when we finally are called by the lock-keepers we join 2 other yachts, one from Cromarty, not far down the Moray Firth, and one from Lossiemouth – Crescent Moon. We spent time chatting with the skipper who told us he was 73! He was sailing with his wife and one crew. Having bought the boat in Bangor, Ireland, they had brought her back across the Irish Sea and were heading home. He was a really interesting guy, who told us he had previously had a Sigma 33 that he had raced for years, but that he had recently struggled to get crew to race her, and he found it too much to handle these days. Crescent Moon is a Hunter Impaler and at 28ft would be much easier to manage for him and his wife.

After tying-up in the Seaport Marina, we walked into Inverness and found the pub by the river Ness, "The Waterside Pub" where we had eaten with Russ on the outbound trip. The pub is very popular with tourists of all kinds and there was an American couple, three cyclists and a Scandinavian family of three, amongst others. The food was very good and reasonably priced, and we enjoyed sitting with our drinks watching the rain falling heavily outside, while the ducks left the river and waddled around on the grass verges. The forecast for tomorrow is not good.

We were therefore surprised the next morning to find the sun shining, a blue sky, and absolutely no wind! From the marina we walked down to the final lock of the canal, the Clachnaharry Lock, to speak to the keeper about "locking out" this morning. The keeper remembered us from the inbound trip (probably the boat's unusual name) and told us that he had been "in trouble" because he hadn't done the paperwork himself that time, but had sent us to the office. One of the girls in the office had apparently resented having to complete our Licence, when it seems it was his job. I felt quite sorry for him as he rushed about in the morning heat dealing with all the boats and their crews and the lock gates, while three personnel sat in comfort in the marina office. Ah well – there's always two sides to every story!

We walked along the canal-side to the entrance into the canal to check the conditions outside the canal. The weather looked set for the day, with no wind and hot sunshine. A pair of herons stood on the opposite bank, ever alert to the possibility of fish, and on our side rabbits ran around in the sun, bobbing in and out of the many holes along the grassy bank. It was a perfect day for mooching about and doing nothing in particular, so that's exactly what we decided to do. The three naval vessels were preparing to leave the canal and head off out to sea with their cadets, and it was quite a spectacle watching them. All hands were at the ready and each of the senior officers kept a watchful eye on their new recruits as they performed their allotted tasks with efficiency. The Sea Lock began to drain and engines were powered-up, the huge lock gates creaked and groaned as they were hydraulically drawn back and the three magnificent naval boats passed out into the Moray Firth.

Steve and I had by now decided to leave tomorrow, weather permitting, and we called in at the marina office to settle-up for electric etc. I walked into Inverness to buy some gifts for the grandchildren (we now have three!) leaving Steve to check out the oil leak and the engine generally – something he would much rather do than go shopping! The afternoon remained hot and sunny and after buying provisions I returned to the boat with some cold beers and a punnet of fresh cherries – delicious! I cooked a pasta dish later that evening and we relaxed on board, watching the comings and goings of other boat users around the marina. Lorna Mohr was still moored-up and Colonel Blimp, as Steve calls him, was marching regimental-style back to his boat, carrying a huge number of bags of shopping, whilst his two crew members trailed behind with a lightweight item each. After a visit to the boatyard and chandlery, we sidled over to the local pub, the Clachnaharry Inn, for a pint or two before retiring for an early night. Steve reminded me that this was where he and his friend Mick went to eat the last time he arrived at the Caledonian Canal with our previous boat Windrift. On that occasion the weather had been quite different, and the food and warmth of the pub had been most welcome.

Inverness to Stonehaven

The following morning we were up early to prepare for departure, and heard a maritime forecast of South-Westerly winds force 3-4: this would be perfect for us, however at the moment there was a clear blue sky, once again, with the sun already bright and no wind whatsoever. The lock keeper advised us that the first gate-opening would be 10.30 am due to the tidal flow, so we passed the time chatting to a couple on the yacht moored next to ours, the Constance. We were surprised to find they came from Whitby, only 20 miles from our home town of Scarborough, because the skipper clearly had a disability that affected his movement and his speech. They had sailed the boat from Whitby and were on their way to Oban, where they had friends who also had a yacht, and that would be their base from now on. He and his wife had previously had a narrow boat on the canals, and had bought a steel hull which they then fitted out themselves! They also had a little dog on board, which he walked around the marina.

When the time came we were called up by the lock-keeper and we went into the lock with another yacht

– Braveheart – crewed by two men who told us they were 84 years of age! These two intrepid sailors were based in Fife and told us they both joined the navy at the age of 18, working on minesweepers. Their visit this time was a sentimental one, as they had been based in Inverness during their navy career. Fishermen for most of their life, they now sailed for relaxation, and chatted knowledgeably about various sailing boats – The Reaper, a sailing barge that we knew from it's frequent visits to Scarborough; The Endeavour, a replica of Captain Cook's ship that we knew from her Whitby base. They knew many of the Scarborough & Whitby fishermen, including our good friend Fred Normandale, and had read his books relating tales of a now vanished, but once vibrant, fishing industry. Steve was curious about the boom set-up on their yacht and was told it was an Aero Rig – very expensive apparently.

By now the water had drained out of the lock and the gates were opened, allowing our boats to motor out into the Beauly Firth and we headed towards the Kessock Bridge. The tidal rips were amazing, swirling round like a washing machine, and the tide was running at 5 knots! Grautvornix was struggling, barely making 2.5 knots against the tide at one point. Suddenly there were two dolphins alongside the boat, swimming against this sweeping tide and racing each other to the bow, then slipping back under the boat, before re-appearing to race back to the bow. I went forward, armed with my camera to try and capture the spectacle, but they are so fast, and although the water was very clear and I took a dozen or more photos, I actually only managed to get one that showed the dolphin clearly. Seals were bobbing-up all over in the Moray Firth, a Tern flew overhead and Cormorants sat atop the Mieke Miele buoy. Steve gave a wide berth to a tug towing some kind of working platform heading down the Firth towards Inverness, then turned astern of him and headed down the buoyed channel marking the edge of the bank. A small tourist-laden vessel was heading towards us on our port side and I, by now on the helm, kept a wary eye on his progress noting that the skipper was talking on the VHF and not looking in our direction. We had right of way and as he came closer I "stood on" and he kept coming, and I stood on – by now all the tourists on his deck and in the saloon, were staring at us uneasily as they drew ever closer. The skipper was clearly oblivious to our presence, until suddenly he looked up and saw us. Quickly he pulled back the throttle and veered away, allowing us to pass on our course, to the great relief of his passengers.

Black clouds were looming and we could see it was raining up ahead, the tide was finally falling away and we gathered speed making 6 knots in the strengthening wind. The day passed quickly and uneventfully and we were soon approaching Lossiemouth Lighthouse on the point and the beacon marking the Halliman Skerries. We had called ahead to the harbour office and been advised to enter the East Basin and go right to the top end of the marina as tomorrow they were expecting the lowest tide for 10 years and we would need the deepest berth to stay afloat. The harbour entrance is hidden when you approach from the west as we were, facing east as it does, and can't be seen until you round the rocks, which is quite unnerving if you sail close-in. We turned Grautvornix into the wind, at a safe distance from the rocks, and took down the sails, starting the engine to power us through the narrow harbour entrance and round into the marina, noting the depth as we went, locating a vacant berth as far up as we could, and tied-up. As it was after 17.00hrs the marina was unmanned, so we headed straight for the Steamboat Inn where we paid for the berth and collected a key to the gate. After a refreshing pint, we walked round the bay to the wooden footbridge that led over the beck to the sand dunes. There was a plaque telling us that the dunes, that provided shelter and a spectacular view, were man-made and that old railway carriages had been used to form the basis of the mound. What imagination!

The last time we were in Lossiemouth we had not managed to find a good place to eat, so we decided to get a Chinese take-away and go back to the boat – bad mistake. It was the worst prawn satay I have ever tasted. They gave us a free bag of prawn crackers and one tin of Coke – why? I prefer wine with my Chinese! Needless to say, the whole lot went in the bin. Fortunately the Lossiemouth Marina provides good services and we enjoyed a hot shower while our clothes went through the wash & dry cycle in the laundry.

The next morning the weather forecast was for a fair wind – NNW 2. The yacht Spring Fever had moored-up next to us and her skipper recognised our boat from Inverness. His name was Chris and he told us he was sailing single-handed around the UK, so we were immediately interested as this is something we intend to do eventually (though not single-handed). Spring Fever was based in Portsmouth and Chris was sailing around clockwise, so had plenty of tales to tell of his journey so far. We chatted and swapped information, he saying he would like to stop-over in Scarborough once we had extolled the virtues of our home port. We asked about his "interesting" self-steering arrangement, which was basically a wind vane, but looked like a broomstick with a bit of metal fastened to it! We all discussed other autohelm set-ups and the many problems we'd had with them. In the meantime the wind was building but we couldn't leave until the tide was favourable, which would be after midday. To make the most of our stay the three of us walked around to the other bay, the West Beach, where the remains of the war defences were visible, and we could see RAF Lossiemouth base across the bay. We studied a memorial to the Stotfield fishing disaster on 25th December 1806 when the whole of the village fishing fleet and crews were lost in a storm.

Arriving back at the boat I prepared lunch, while Chris prepared Spring Fever for departure – she drew less than Grautvornix, so could get out a little earlier. The wind was very strong now and Steve & I offered to let his ropes off, making it (theoretically) easier for him to reverse out of the berth. On his word, we cast off the ropes. A sudden gust blew the bow round and his only option was to reverse all the way down the marina channel to a turning point. We watched in amazement as our new friend showed us what he is made of, batting not an eyelid, as they say, at this new challenge. We raced up to the sea wall to watch him leave the harbour entrance, eager to know what the conditions were like out in the open sea before we had to make the journey. I had the wind meter with me and the gusts were up to 20mph. Spring Fever struggled against the wind and waves, and it seemed ages before he had the sails set and was off on his way. We decided to wait another half an hour – surely this wind would abate – the forecast had not mentioned this! So we went back to the boat and Steve lay on his bunk and went to sleep. I sat and tried to read – but I couldn't concentrate – I kept thinking of what lay ahead and just basically sat and worried.

At 15.00hrs we left Lossiemouth. The wind meter was showing gusts of 14mph, which was a little better, but the sea had now built to a big swell. The exit from the harbour mouth was difficult and swilly. I helmed and Steve put up a reefed mainsail. We made 7 knots all the way, the sea finally easing a little, but still very swilly – it was all too much for me and I sat and cowered under the spray hood, except for taking the helm each time Steve needed to adjust the sails. We arrived Whitehills at 19.30hrs. Chris was standing on the sea wall in the full force of the wind, waiting for us! He had wanted to take a photo of us coming in, so that we could see what it was like – something you can't do yourself of course, and I was most impressed with the photo when I saw it – the conditions looked just as bad as I had imagined. Chris had had a problem with his boat's furling gear and told us he had spent 2 hours laid at the bow fixing it – which gave us another insight into the character of this amazing man. The wind had been Force 6 and there had been a 3 meter swell all the time he was carrying out these repairs.

Our boats were now tied-up on the pontoons of the outer harbour, and so was Hilary Lister's boat "Me Too", with her support boat. We had heard about Hilary's marvellous sailing achievements so were very excited to see she was here. Hilary is paralysed from the neck down and sails alone in a boat specially designed for her, which she steers by a sophisticated system of "sip & puff". My former employer, Pindar plc, had helped her acquire the boat and sponsored her sail across the channel some time ago, so I was particularly interested to see the vessel.

The three of us walked up the hill to the Cutty Restaurant where we had a very nice fish pie. We had a curious "going on" prior to eating, though, as we asked in the bar for a table for three. There was much shaking of heads as we were told that the restaurant was full – it being Saturday night. Then after some cajoling they agreed to squeeze us in, taking us upstairs to a rather nice room. We were therefore puzzled to find that there were several empty tables that remained empty for the rest of the evening. I had a sleepless night that night as the wind howled and the swell rocked the boat on its mooring, and every now and then she lurched hard on her "spring". At one point during the night Steve was visible up on top of the coach-roof in his undies, trying to secure flapping halyards, but the noise persisted after he came back to bed. The cause of the sound was finally identified as a rogue metal coat-hanger in the wet-locker!

Saturday 25th July brought a slightly calmer day, the sea conditions having improved and the swell much less than the day before. The wind forecast was NW 3-

4 going 3-0 variable – later SE 5-6. I was a little unsure after our experience on previous occasions, but Steve left the decision whether or not to leave today to me. I made up my mind as soon as I saw Hilary Lister's support crew getting her boat ready to leave – if Hilary was going, so was I! After a swilly start the sea flattened off nicely and we had blue sky and sunshine all the way, plus the benefit of 4 knots of tide going with us around Rattray Head – a notorious stretch of water where several tidal-flows meet. We had the wind behind us and were making 9 knots at times – a huge relief for me after yesterday. En route we heard the Forth & Aberdeen Coastguard calling Macduff Lifeboat on channel 16 – there was no response, but we had passed the lifeboat going in the other direction towards Whitehills a little earlier. The coastguard then called for any other boats in Whitehills harbour – no response. We were intrigued, but shortly after that a couple of yachts responded saying they were close by. We heard later on the local radio in Peterhead that the body of a man had been found in Whitehills harbour. It seems there is no VHF radio signal inside the harbour.

We made Peterhead Bay by 16.00hrs – Spring Fever had left before us and we saw him sailing in the distance, arriving soon after us. Hilary Lister arrived a couple of hours later and her mother was on the pontoon waiting for her having driven the motor home that serves as Hilary's accommodation at each stop-over. As Hilary came alongside the pontoon in Me Too, her support crew lifted her out of the special seat on her boat and into her wheelchair. We watched from our berth close by as preparations were made to transfer her to her waiting motor home and her boat was made secure. I tried to imagine what it must be like to be so reliant on others for almost everything, and this helped me to understand the joy she experienced in lone sailing. However, knowing what she must have endured recently, sailing through rough seas and bad weather, we resisted the urge to go over and chat so that she could be whisked away to rest without delay.

It was Saturday night and the Peterhead Big Weekend was well underway. A large marquee had been erected on the green in the bay and young local bands were playing. We wandered over later and enjoyed a beer outside in the sunshine – there was food available too: a choice of burgers or char-grilled local kippers. No contest – we shared a delicious kipper. The bands were not bad – it reminded us of our boys when they were younger and we frequently drove them & their equipment to their gigs, waiting patiently (and proudly) to drive them home again. Back on the boat we watched other boat users as they all got on with various activities in the summer evening sun. There were two Dutch yachts moored close by, both with families on board. A young boy of about 8 years was rowing his younger sister in a dinghy, and rowing very well, completely in control. He brought the dinghy alongside the pontoons, tied her off and deftly tied two lengths of rope together with a perfect bowline!

I cooked on board that evening, not wanting to experience the dubious delights of Peterhead town centre, and we soon began to feel weary. At 9.30 with the music still in full swing in the marquee we gave in and went to bed. We were to sleep through a fantastic firework display, completely oblivious to the noise!

The following morning was a different picture. The marquee was empty, with bottles and other debris strewn about the grassy bank, and the rain was heavy, with a strong wind blowing. The forecast was SE 4/5 and after short consideration we decided to stay put for another day. We had the luxury of a long hot shower and a lazy breakfast, listening to the local radio station that played an excellent selection of music that morning: Deacon Blue, James Morrison, The Waterboys, Jack Johnson, David Bowie, Scouting For Boys etc, etc. It was a good day to read books. Later we decided to walk to the cliff top at the point, so that we could assess the sea conditions. The path took us from the marina up a steep incline to the large building that had intrigued us, perched as it was on top of the cliff with what must be a wonderful view, but it had no windows. It soon became obvious that it was a prison. We felt distinctly uncomfortable as we took the only path to the cliff edge that ran around the fence surrounding the prison walls, equipped with CCTV cameras at every turn. The view out to sea confirmed what we had thought, today was not a day to go sailing for fun! We caught a bus into the town centre and, being a wet Sunday, were not really surprised that the place was almost deserted, with the exception of the odd dubious character hanging around looking suspicious. The town is fairly grim, with hard & charmless architecture. There was nothing open – and if they had been open, I doubt we would have gone into any of the coffee bars. We walked back along the road that runs between the town and the marina, calling at the shop attached to the local petrol station. There was a pizza take-away on the same site, and I checked the opening times in the hope of being able to get pizzas for tea that night – it was closed until tomorrow so we went into the shop for supplies. We got the basics and went to the till to pay. The prices amused us – there were two prices on each item: one for pre 10pm and another for post 10pm purchases!

The weather forecasts from various sources were contradictory – it seemed there were several fronts battling for supremacy and no-one could give a definitive forecast. We obtained one from Chris, who had his computer on board, that said SW 3 / 4, whereas the coastguards were giving SW 4/5 going Force 6. There was much discussion and head scratching over what to expect tomorrow, and we finally gave-up the speculation, ate on the boat, and later walked back into Peterhead town centre with Chris for a couple of beers before retiring. He was great company and the three of us had no shortage of conversation, finding all sorts of common interests. These included house renovation projects, which we were delighted to talk about, having recently completed a five-storey Georgian house restoration that had been uninhabitable when we bought it. Chris had done a similar renovation and we swapped all the usual tales of finding "horrors" as you went along!

Monday morning and we awoke to wind, rain and (for July) a chilly temperature. The VHF forecast at 07.00hrs gave winds of SW force 4/5, which I was beginning to get used to! As Green Day sang "21 Guns" on the radio, we debated our next move and decided to leave for Stonehaven at 12.00hrs and go with the tide. We should be there in 6 hours and arriving around 18.00hrs would give us plenty of daylight and we would have time to find somewhere ashore to have our evening meal. What a day we were in for. We had the heaviest rain I've ever seen, a roaring thunderstorm and at one point huge hailstones rained down on us! When we set sail there was a long lazy swell and we chose to set the main with one reef, so that we could either take it out, if the wind eased, or put in a second reef if it freshened. Out at sea we were sailing well and watching the changing sky, which anyone who cruises will know is imperative in order to anticipate weather conditions. We watched in amazement as the storm gathered in the distance and spread across the sky towards us – the colours were incredible: navy-blue sky and a bright turquoise sea. I wanted desperately to take a photograph, but once again I'd left my camera below and it was far too rough to contemplate going for it, and good job I didn't. There was a sudden and immediate ninety-degree wind-shift, with absolutely no warning, that sent the boom crash-jibing across the boat. The wind was blowing force 5/6 which meant it went with quite a force and the boat heeled over so violently that the port-side gunwales were completely submerged! Steve once again proved his sailing skills as he held tight control of the tiller whilst simultaneously letting out the mainsheet, so that the boat self-righted and we were not thrown into the sea. This was no mean feat as it was all done at right-angles to the boat and with enormous pressure on the main sheet, requiring both quick reactions and super strength. It is at times like these that I am in complete admiration of the likes of Ellen MacArthur who must have such strength to accomplish Around The World sailing trips. I could barely hold on to the boat for dear life, never mind actually do something about the situation!

This all happened just as we were enjoying our "grab-food" – a couple of sandwiches that I had made earlier – and as Steve had one hand on the tiller and a sandwich in the other, something had to give. The sandwich was flung un-ceremoniously overboard. Once the storm had passed over, the sea began to calm down and I took over the helm. Steve was by now quite exhausted. We were passing Aberdeen and there were endless helicopters passing overhead, one after another – no doubt supply aircraft for the oil platforms – and many big ships at anchor. I had a scary moment when one of the ships, that I had assumed was at anchor, turned round to face us! I had adjusted our course to give room to the vessel, just in case, but it seemed very close. Of course it was just the tide moving it round. A very long six hours and finally we sighted Stonehaven. The Almanac had informed us that we would be mooring against the wall in the outer harbour, where there was plenty of water at all states of the tide, so we went in expectantly with throwing ropes at the ready on both port and starboard sides. There was an elderly man shouting and waving for us to follow his direction, so we approached the wall as directed and as I made to throw a rope to him, he picked up a heavy mooring rope that was already tied to underwater chains and proceeded to hurl it across. I caught it, but it was clear the thick salty-hard rope would never fit round our cleats. The wind was all the time trying to blow us back, away from the wall, and I had to drop the rope and shout to the man to catch our boat's own mooring ropes, before disaster struck – you know the kind: where you're suddenly out of control due to tiredness and confusion, and worst of all, through somebody interfering with a good plan! He did apologise later, and his intentions were good, but we discovered he wasn't the harbour man but another boat owner. His own boat was a beautiful-looking wooden yacht, intriguingly named "Brunhilda", with a very strange steering arrangement – he stood in a hole cut into the deck. When we commented that there seemed to be no drainage system in said hole, he explained quite simply "I have a scoop and bail her out". Even stranger – they had been around the Shetland Isles and his wife was also sailing with him and their 5 cats! He told us that he had built the boat in 1974 from 1 ton of mahogany, in his home port of Edinburgh.

It was low water and we had quite a climb from the boat up a very "iffy" rope ladder to the quayside, where we had our first glimpse of the pretty little harbour-side town of Stonehaven. The natural bay provided a lovely haven for the locals and their boats. There was an inner harbour for the local boat owners, protected from even the worst winter storm by a substantial stone wall and with a retractable boon for the entrance that can be put in place when the storm winds are forecast to blow directly at it. The mooring fee was cheap enough at £15 per night, however the facilities consisted of a public toilet and a disabled toilet that had a shower. Just the one.

Chris in Spring Fever and Hilary Lister in Me Too both arrived sometime later and Chris joined us in the

Ship Inn for seafood pasta and lots of beer! We spent a very pleasant evening in the summer sunshine outside the Inn, watching the locals and the holiday makers enjoying the sand and the sea and swapping stories of our day. Steve best described the day's weather conditions when he commented we had had "four seasons in one day". Chris, being the amazing sailor that he is, had managed amid the storm's lashing, to grab his camera and capture the colours of the sea and sky, whilst still managing to keep his boat on course.

The next leg of our journey was to be from Stonehaven to Eyemouth and we arose early as usual to check the weather forecast broadcast on the VHF at 07.30 hrs: S-SW Force 4/5 going 5/7 later. Ouch! It was Blue sky and sunshine first thing and we walked into town for provisions, then up to the top of the cliff to the war memorial where we could get a good view of the sea conditions. The waves were breaking over white occasionally though there was no big swell, but I was none too happy with the forecast. When we arrived back at the harbour, the TV cameraman on the Hilary Lister assignment was there and we chatted with him about their plans for that day. He told us he had had problems with his equipment yesterday, due to the weather, and also that Hilary was having a rest-day today, to recover. Hilary was featured in that day's Press & Journal and her progress was being tracked on television's "The One Show". We then went to find the harbourmaster, a very friendly chap, who advised us not to go today. Shortly after that the heavens opened again and the rain became torrential, just as Spring Fever was departing, and Steve got absolutely drenched as he helped Chris cast-off his ropes. I was sitting snugly in a café over-looking the harbour, and he dashed in dripping all over the floor. I had ordered coffee & sandwiches, which we tucked into whilst agreeing with each other that we had made the right decision to stay-over. We finished our lunch and were idly chatting, waiting for Steve to dry-out, when his mobile went – it was Chris. He had got as far as the point and decided to turn back – there was little or no wind to sail, and the rain caused such poor visibility it was like a white-out! Chris shouted down the phone "this is supposed to be a holiday! I can't sail because what little wind there is, is in the wrong direction – plus I can't see a thing for the rain! I'm coming back" Another drenching for Steve as he dashed out to catch the ropes.

Back on board Grautvornix we read the papers with interest as Hilary's trip was a featured article, then took a walk through the town and around the bay. By late afternoon the forecast wind still had not come and Steve was wishing we had gone today after all, but our plan now was to leave Stonehaven on the early tide in the morning (05.00hrs – oh joy!). The latest 24 hour forecast was still showing wind at force 6/7 at times. Meanwhile I had a text from our friend Graham in Fort Augustus telling us he had been out "paddling" last night and the only time he got wet was when he got out of the water! Another text came in from Win, our friend and the Commodore's wife back in Scarborough, to tell me that I was her "hero" – this obviously referred to the fact that I had not got on the first available train home after the first storm!

We had tea on the boat and later went to the Ship Inn with Chris, where we once again enjoyed a couple of beers and some good stories. Chris told us of the time he decided to do a Stand-up Comedy Course, culminating in a performance in a theatre in Leicester Square – what a man!

The wind finally came during the night and we spent a very swilly night on board, with the boat bouncing about and Steve re-positioning the fenders several times. Needless to say we didn't leave at 5am as planned. At 07.30 hrs the rain had stopped and the sun came out – which I was glad of, because the condensation in the sleeping quarters had made the bedding damp, and I took advantage of the chance to air the bedding over the boom in the sunshine. Steve went for a shower, and as I said, the facilities were basically just a key to the disabled toilet. Unfortunately when Steve unlocked the door and went in, there was an enormously fat man sitting naked on the toilet. Not a good sight first thing in the morning. The harbourmaster said he had been trying to get better facilities, but was so far unsuccessful, although there was feasibility study on the cards for installing pontoons, but this would involve putting dock-gates on the inner harbour.

Chris came over with his lap-top to look at the various weather sites with us – we all three sat in the bus-shelter as the wi-fi reception was best there – good job as it happened as the rain came again, and heavily too. It looked as though tomorrow would be better. Resigned to another night ashore, we headed off to the cliff top where we could see a memorial of some kind, and way beyond, the remains of a castle. The walk was glorious, with barley fields spread-out on both sides that were clearly the inspiration for Sting's composition "Fields of Gold". The memorial was commemorating all those who fought for their country in various wars, and was spectacularly placed so that, standing in the middle, one had a panoramic view of the landscape from sea to sky and everything in-between. Our walk then took us along the cliff edge, following the contours of the land, and down to the start of the long stretch of stone steps that led to the castle entrance. Dunnator Castle was built high atop a sheer cliff face and is the most amazing feat of stone-masonry, having several parts to it that must have taken many years to build. Ponies were used to carry the supplies up the steep steps, and the stable block where they were kept is still standing. We were able to stand and imagine life in this environment – there was evidence of the kitchen garden, the pond & well where the water supply came from, the inevitable church, and even the stone cells where prisoners would have been kept – complete with drain-hole in the sloping floor where their "slops" would have self-emptied! A plaque recorded that William Wallace had stayed there. Modern life now mixed with the history as visitors roamed the site – we had to pass a Spanish tourist on the entrance steps whose mobile phone was glued to his ear while he held a very loud conversation with someone. It was, however, a pleasure to note that the owners of the site, although it was now a tourist attraction, had not felt the need to spoil it with café, burger bar, ice-cream stand, souvenir shop, or anything that would detract from the authentic atmosphere. Even the necessary toilets were discreetly included in stone buildings that blended perfectly into the rest of the site.

We had noticed the teeming sea-bird colonies on the cliffs below Dunnator Castle and when we arrived back at the harbour, one of the locals, whose boat we were admiring, told us that he had been commissioned by Sky TV to take a film crew out to the colonies. The trip had had to be postponed due to the sea conditions, and his alternative activity that afternoon, calibrating the compass of an ROV (Remote Operated Vehicle), was also not going to happen due to the "lumpy" sea. You think you are in a quiet little seaport where nothing really happens, and when you look a little closer – it's all going on! Or not – as was the case that day.

It was a lovely evening and we noticed that a lot of dinghy sailors were getting their boats ready to go out. Watching from the shore, behind the little café, we realised there was to be club racing that night and looked forward to spectating. While all the boats were assembling around the start mark, we observed the Race Officer, who apparently had a post behind the little café, that consisted of a small lock-up container, with all the race boards, flags, binoculars, chairs and other paraphernalia. The Race Boards were to be hung on hooks in the wall of the café, which was only accessible by climbing over an uneven surface of rocks. The Race Officer that day seemed to be acting alone, and, not the most agile of men, was really struggling to lift the huge boards into place. Being involved in yacht racing at home, we knew how important his job was to the race entrants who needed to see the boards to know what the course was that day. Steve went over to ask if he could help, and from that moment on we were both nominated assistant race officers! The poor man was trying to run the race himself, when at least three people were needed. There were over 30 competitors, comprising both dinghies and lazers, and they required a race starter, a race finisher, a results recorder, and a race-rules monitor throughout. You needed three pairs of eyes to keep track of all the boats going round the marks, and when the finish came it was a mammoth task to identify each boat as it crossed the finish line, sound the air-horn to let them know they were "over", and mark down the sail number and finish time on the results board. It was frantic! However, job done and the man was hugely relieved, however he then revealed that he had also been asked to organise supper for everyone – fish & chips all round – but when he had remembered and phoned the chip shop, they were closed! He would definitely not be popular when everyone came in from the sea expecting a hot supper! Sadly we couldn't help with that.

After our little adventure, we walked over to the pub for a couple of beers with Chris and then retired for an early night. Late that evening a small motor-sailor – Catch 22 – came in and rafted-up alongside Grautvornix. The single-handed skipper told us he had been out to the Shetlands and was on passage back to Amble, his home port. He asked where we were from and said he knew several of the Scarborough Yacht Club members, having taken part in the North Sea Race aboard "The Parrot" (as we know it – remembered as such because of the owner's habit of wearing a stuffed toy parrot on his shoulder). Small world.

His boat kept us awake most of the night with the swell pushing and heaving it up against the fenders, which squeaked and squealed with the pressure.

Stonehaven to Blythe

Imagine our delight when the alarm sounded at 04.00hrs after a sleepless night – we heaved ourselves out of the bunk and prepared to leave Stonehaven. By 05.00hrs we were on our way – Catch 22 had already cast-off his ropes and gone, as had Spring Fever, but having a deeper draft, we had to wait for a little more water. As we left the harbour, there was a strange banging noise coming from the stern. I got all the fenders in, stowed the mooring ropes and we took the revs off to listen. Steve held the rudder fast as the rolling motion of the sea tried to turn us off course, and I lifted the lid of the stern locker where the noise had come from: "what's the thick black pipe do?" I shouted over the wind. "It's the exhaust!" shouted back Steve. The bracket had broken, leaving the pipe banging about inside the locker, and we would have to fix it before going any further. After half an hour of laying upside-down with his head in the locker, Steve had secured the pipe and we set off once again. With the wind blowing a strong westerly we sailed with the jib and a reef in the main-sail and soon we were making

6/7 knots. Yippee! This was looking good – the sky was clearing-out to reveal blue patches, with white fluffy clouds. The sea was "slight" to begin with, then progressed to "moderate" – I have no idea who dreamed-up the criteria for the title of the sea conditions, but my "moderate" is nothing like the seaman's term! Anyway, for seafaring people it was moderate, for everyone else it was rough! By the time we were passing the Firth of Forth entrance the sea had grown to a really big swell (not a technical term but most people will know what that means!) and the wind could be accurately described as "fresh". More precisely it was gusting up to Force 7 and the swell was 4 meters, making the last two hours of the journey quite a challenge, in fact we were twice blown broadsides and had to take the mainsail down. This as usual involved me helming into the wind, which was difficult when all the elements were trying desperately to turn us around the other way. I was forced to throw the throttle forward to full revs several times in order to push against the wind and waves, holding her steady so that Steve could haul down the sail, and manhandle it into some sort of shape in order to get the ties round and stop it from being blown completely off the boom. My hero, once again. I, meanwhile, was concentrating very hard on not being petrified. At one point Spring Fever called us over the VHF and I responded but couldn't hear his reply, due to signal problems. He had decided to carry on past Arbroath and go to Eyemouth. We passed Catch 22 on the same course as us.

The Gannets were out in force that day and to my joy I had the privilege of witnessing 15 of them flying in a line – 7 pairs and a juvenile, all out fishing, whilst below them the guillemots and puffins skittered about on the surface with the same aim. Eventually the conditions became so bad that we had to take down the jib and fire-up the engine – it was just too dangerous to sail. Every now and then a huge wave would rise up and engulf the boat, soaking us to the skin. We had closed the cockpit hatch to try and keep the boat dry on the inside, and it had been far too rough to risk going below anyway, which meant that we spent the whole day without food. At 15.00hrs we arrived at Eyemouth, and having left at 05.00, it had seemed a very long day. Spring Fever came into sight and arrived about the same time, and Catch 22 arrived about an hour later.

The next day Steve revealed what he had been thinking that day. He had studied the clouds and seen angry monsters in them – half pig, half poodle, with angry faces! Looking into this phenomenon later, via the Reed's Almanac, I discovered that the cloud formation was identified as "Cumulonimbus" and the narrative read "hazardous to yachts"!

Meanwhile, we tied up to the pontoon, cold, wet, tired & starving, while Chris, rafting-up Spring Fever next to us, shouted: "what a fantastic sail!" (we just knew he would say that) – whilst we had decided it was an endurance test, he had actually taken a slightly different course and sailed closer to the coast, getting at least a little shelter, and having himself a wonderful time!

Eyemouth is a big fishing port, with many boats & trawlers – some of them huge, and all with Philippino crew. There is a big fish market and a maritime museum, shaped to look like a galleon's stern. We amused ourselves for a while looking at all the boats, Chris and I noted that the name of the boat moored next to us was only one letter short of a woman's body part – until we found out later it was the name of an island off Mull – Ulva. The three of us walked along the jetty to the port offices and found the harbourmaster's office – he was a salty old sea-dog with a gruff hard-lived voice and funny eyes. He asked our boat's name and on hearing it remarked loudly "In my day boats used to have pretty names like "Morning Star" or "Autumn Rose" not bloody German rubbish!" And I thought to myself: yes and names like "Our Maggie" and "Our Lass" – great! Although the building was relatively new, the facilities, yet again, had no laundry. The harbourmaster, whom I shall call "Oor Tammy", just because it seemed to fit, recommended the Ship Inn for good seafood, and because we knew no better, we headed around the quay to said pub. We walked into the grubbiest, shabbiest bar I had yet to encounter, ordered a beer and immediately had our doubts about the suitability of this place for serving food. The seating around the edge of the bar was ripped, with the foam cushion oozing out, and the carpet was just filthy. The barmaid was very friendly and supplied us with good beer and a tempting menu – and before we could object, she was ushering us behind the bar which, bizarrely, was the way to the restaurant. Pushing us through a door we found ourselves in a completely different scene – a pleasant, well set-out dining room, bustling with customers and alive with delicious smells. Maybe this was not such a bad idea after all!

After a delicious Seafood Medley and a couple of beers we all three had faces that showed we were warm, well-fed, well-watered and well and truly weathered. The only thing we needed now was sleep, and we retired early to do just that, my last wish before dozing-off being for a better forecast for tomorrow.

Little did I know we were in for quite a frustrating day on the Friday that we planned to leave Eyemouth. We waited for the 07.30 coastguard's forecast on the VHF and motored out of the harbour at 08.00 hours, leaving Chris to spend a day ashore to recover from his hard sail yesterday. The forecast was for a SE wind Force 3 to 4 – going 5 to 6. As we reached open water the wind was Westerly Force 2 and the sea-state slight, and we put up the main-sail, with a cautionary reef, and the jib. By the time we approached Berwick-on-Tweed we were sailing really well. Making good progress we were soon passing Lindisfarne and the Farne Islands, with seals popping their heads up out of the water to nosey at us. We could see the white sandy beaches and the castles of the Holy Island and Bamburgh. But soon we were slowing and the tide was turning, there was not enough wind to push us against the tide, even after taking the reef out of the main-sail. Our frustration grew as we put the engine on, but no sooner had we got into motor-sailing, than the wind shifted to the South-East and picked-up to a Force 3-4 and we had to put the reef back into the main. We took down the jib and struggled to keep up the speed as the wind continued to shift directions and the sea conditions were holding us back – trying our best not to "bang down" on the waves as they lifted the bow then dropped it as the wave fell away. Wind against tide does not make for comfortable sailing. Tacking & jibing constantly we tried to get the most out of the main. We could see in the distance the chimneys of Newbiggin, but it was taking forever to get there and we fervently wished we had left earlier to get the most of the tide that morning. The last two hours of the journey seemed to take forever and we had both had enough – Steve was worn out with the constant sail-changes and the exhaust-pipe problem that had occurred again, which he sorted-out en route, and I was just worn-out with all the normal things you have to do on a boat that become such hard work in difficult conditions. Things like checking the chart and the plotter, throwing together food & drinks to keep us going, and going to the loo, which is in itself an almighty effort!

Still it was never so bad that we didn't appreciate the things around us, like the dozens of puffins off Croquet Island sitting on the water and twittering, the whole flock parting as the boat's bow approached – a few flying off with their little wings flapping like mad to get into the air. On passage we heard the coastguard on channel 16 saying they were sending the lifeboat out to a boat in trouble off Amble, followed by a call from Catch 22 informing the coastguard that he was within sight of the boat and would go to their assistance. The skipper of Catch 22 then called again about 15 minutes later to say he had them under tow, heading towards Amble. What a cool dude – he's a hero!

At last the wind turbines of Blythe were in sight. It was 19.00hrs before we got the sails down and motored into Blythe harbour, exhausted after 11 hours at sea. The visitor's pontoon was full, but the boats had tied-up carelessly and we had to ask a couple of their skippers to move up for us, which they did gracefully. I cooked us a hot meal and was totally prepared to just fall into bed, when Steve announced we should pay a visit to the Yacht Club – despite my protests to the contrary, that is what we did. Blythe yacht club is sited on a converted boat in the harbour, and although it was a little damp and smelly (diesel-smell) the members in the bar were very friendly and chatted to us. We eventually returned to the boat and fell into bed, thoroughly exhausted, at 11.30pm.

During the night the wind was wild and we awoke to a very wet & windy day. The forecast that morning confirmed we were not going anywhere that day – and we sat in the saloon listening to the wind turbines whizzing round and wondering how long this weather would last. We were running out of time. Our plan had been to return to our home port of Scarborough by Friday 31st of July and that was yesterday, although we had some leeway, we both needed to be back at work on Monday and, today being Saturday, we were still a long way from home in sailing terms. My mother rang later that day to say her friend had died suddenly.

Saturday 1st August 2009 and it's my eldest son Danny's birthday. I can't believe it's 33 years since the day he was born, and I spent a few minutes remembering how proud I was to have my first son. I was sorry I wasn't around for his birthday, though I did expect a quip from him about not being there for his birthday for the second time in his life (private joke). He sent me a text with a photo of his new son Max in his bouncy-harness – lovely! I am really missing everyone now after a month away and I need to be home soon. To be sure to keep in touch with everyone I then sent a text to my younger son Tom, who was busy in the recording studio. He later rang to say he had his son Jacob staying for the week. I rang my sister Alison, she regaled me with tales of her recently acquired Jack Russell puppy "Jack" trying to eat a blackbird and humping a dachshund at puppy class – priceless.

Steve and I had a slow start, cooking breakfast and taking a shower after washing the boat down. We walked into Blythe town for provisions – a grim place with not much going for it at first glance. The shops were limited and we noted you could only buy things in twos – there seemed to be no single items for sale. As we waited at the check-out I noticed the stand displaying cheap vodka at £5 per bottle and cans of own-brand Red Bull type drink to go with it – you can get out of your head here for a fiver! Oh joy. Our return walk revealed a better side of Blythe as we headed back via the new quayside and boardwalk, and through a park. The park was lovely, with two greens for bowls, tennis courts and many gated-off children's adventure playgrounds, plus a water-feature play area that looked great fun. What a surprise after seeing the rest of the town that looked soul-less and depressing. It transpired that Lottery Funding had made possible this improvement to the area – what a great thing to spend our money on – keep buying the tickets!

The afternoon was spent chilling-out on the boat, me listening to the radio (The Script, David Gray, Damien Rice etc) and Steve looking at all the other boats and measuring the wind speed. It was averaging 8mph but gusting up to 16mph. Friends were texting us with weather forecasts and offering us lifts back to Scarborough if we had to leave the boat – how good is that?! We finally got a good forecast from both Chris and Fiona – South Westerly Force 4/5 going Westerly Force 3 /4. Fantastic – that meant we could leave tomorrow! We made the boat ready and went down to the yacht club for scampi & chips and a couple of beers to celebrate. There were several local members in the club bar and we listened to their conversations with interest. They chatted about their sailing experiences and their trips – most had been to Ijmuiden and the inland waters of Holland and the Netherlands. It seemed everyone here was called Dave....

The Homeward Leg

The alarm went at 06.45 hours, we had a quick breakfast and slipped the mooring ropes, and I called up channel 12 and requested permission to depart Blythe Harbour. The Harbour Office reported all clear to leave and we hoisted the main and the jib as we entered the bay. The sea was smooth and the wind was gusting force 4/5 and Steve took the helm for a while, handing over to me as the wind gradually dropped to force 3. The VHF radio was surprisingly active, with all the lifeboats out up and down the coast for their regular Sunday morning exercises. As we ran down the coastline I enjoyed identifying the towns and cities along the way – Tynemouth, Newcastle, North & South Shields, Sunderland, Hartlepool, Redcar, and Saltburn. The Gannets were diving for fish and were as spectacular as ever. Large shipping was moving in and out of Hartlepool and huge ferries sweeping into Newcastle. It was great to be sailing again – and on the smooth sea we were making 7 knots!

With such good progress, soon we were passing Boulby, with the huge chimney of the potash mine, and then Staithes and our most favourite place: Runswick Bay.

Suddenly over the VHF we heard a familiar call – one of our dive club boats! Bellraiser had a casualty and was calling the coastguard, who alerted the sea-rescue helicopter. The casualty was then transferred to another of our club member's boats – Empress – and a third dive boat, Francis Anne, was calling Bellraiser. It was very worrying and certainly frustrating, hearing it all going on and not being able to assist. With the binoculars we could see the helicopter hovering over the boats just off Whitby, and winching-up, it seemed very close to the surface of the water and seemed to last for ever. Then suddenly it was gone. We tried to call our friends on Francis Anne but there was no response. We later learned that one of the young members of our diving club had had a rapid assent and suspected a possible "Bend". He turned out to be OK and no harm done, luckily. The Scarborough Sub Aqua Club has an excellent safety record, which we attribute to the quality of the training programme and the safe diving practices, so it was with great sadness that we heard a week later of the death while diving of one of our most experienced divers, Colin Bell.

As we sailed around Whitby headland our final goal slowly came into view – the castle on the very distinctive Scarborough headland. We were nearly home and could hardly contain our excitement as we raced along clocking-up the final miles. The wind stayed with us and we were having possibly the best day's sailing of the whole trip! At 17.00hrs we were sailing across the most familiar North Bay, passing the Sea Life Centre and the new Sands development, along the whole stretch of the Marine Drive, built with enormous foresight by Victorian engineers, and rounding the castle headland, avoiding the many fishing marker-buoys, and passing the pleasure cruiser the Regal Lady, who sounded her ship's horn as if to welcome us home. Into the South Bay we sailed and turned Grautvornix into the wind, pulled down the sails and started the engine, fastening on the fenders as we motored through the harbour mouth and made for our berth. As we approached the berth, there was an enthusiastic "whoop" from our welcoming committee aboard the yacht Tamurey opposite – what a nice surprise! Our friends had gathered for the usual "Sunday Social" aboard Colin's yacht and were just in time to see us arrive. They all shouted for us to join them and Steve couldn't wait – but I held back. It was hard for me after a 10 hour solitary-sail and 4 weeks of peaceful days to drop back into the middle of a party. I needed time to adjust, but it wasn't to be, and I took a deep breath and followed Steve along the pontoons to the waiting crowd of well-wishers, all wanting to hear about our trip. I would have to wait just a little longer before I could unlock our front door and feel that I was home at last.

Several days later we had a call from our new friend Chris of "Spring Fever". He had decided to stop-over in Scarborough on his way down the coast and we rushed down to the harbour to greet him. Chris had arranged for his sister-in-law Georgina to join him in Scarborough and sail with him on the next leg of his journey homeward, so we were only too happy to meet her and the four of us booked a table at the local

Italian restaurant, overlooking the harbour. We three intrepid sailors re-told all our tales, with a fair amount of exaggeration involved, and George sat patiently listening and laughing with us (at least I think it was with us, not at us!) After the meal, Chris & George retired early, planning to set alarms for 5am and sail on the morning tide, so we said our good-byes and promised to keep in touch. It wasn't to be "good-bye" so soon. As they made to leave the harbour at 6am Chris put the engine into gear – and went nowhere. No forward thrust, no reverse thrust. They were floating in the middle of the harbour with no drive power. Fortunately there was only a little wind, and Chris managed to float the boat to the nearest pontoon, where he tied her up and scratched his head. "Must be something in the prop" he muttered "I'll put on a wetsuit and go and investigate". Sliding off the pontoon into the water he unfortunately found that someone had had a diesel spillage, and it was not at all pleasant bobbing beneath the surface. Peering underneath the stern of the boat he immediately saw what the problem was – the propeller was no longer attached! There was nothing there at all to propel the boat – no wonder she had not responded to the frantic revving of the engine! It transpired that inferior bolts had been used to secure the prop and they had simply sheared off. The upshot of this was that he and George would be able to sample the delights of the Scarborough area for a couple of days whilst they waited for the necessary parts and for the repairs to be carried out. When they finally got away poor George had only a short sail down to Grimsby, where she had to disembark and rush off to catch a plane, booked for a long-planned family holiday. Chris carried on alone and, as he told us later, had an uneventful final leg back to his home port. He contacted us some time later with a copy of the book he had written of his trip – what a lovely surprise, not only because we featured in it, but because we could now read about the bits before and after we joined him! The only thing I was slightly "miffed" about was that he had beaten me to finish writing his story....

However, the friendship continues as Chris has asked Steve & I to crew for him on the next Round The Island Race – which we're very keen to do. So watch this space!

Meanwhile Steve and I slipped back into our daily lives and things returned to normal. We occasionally run our photos as a slideshow on the computer, just to remind ourselves of the trip and to keep the memory fresh. What a great experience it was! What a lot we learned, and more importantly, what a lot of fun we had!

Postscript

It isn't everyone that gets the opportunity to make a bid for freedom and I consider myself one of the lucky ones. I count amongst these opportunities my many diving trips, a couple of long distance cycle rides and to date two yacht-cruising adventures, and I have loved every one of them. Being out at sea, away from all the normal daily routines and responsibilities, away from all the noise, the traffic, the crowds, and everything that pulls one from the things one would really prefer to be doing, is without doubt the best feeling in the world. I suppose this is the way of life in the so-called "developed world". The inhabitants of many of the "undeveloped" countries of the world have this freedom and think nothing of it, but to us it is most precious. We spend our young lives learning how to play the game of working, earning, spending, saving, planning for the future – only to spend the latter half of our lives learning how to relax and enjoy the simple things in life. How often do most ordinary people go out and do something that doesn't require a car, a telephone, a computer or a television, or any kind of technical gadget, for that matter? How many of us teach our children to recognise a bird's call, or take them to sit under the stars for the night? If we can find a space in the open with no light pollution, that is! We are all too busy living our lives in order to make enough money to afford a holiday, that ends up being a week sitting on a beach in Spain, because either we think that's what the children need, or we ourselves are too tired to contemplate anything more adventurous.

I am lucky enough to have met many people, now close friends, who want to share in all the kind of activities that give me a sense of the freedom that I talk about.

On this sailing trip my husband Steve and I have relished every sight and sound of nature that we encountered; have marvelled at the stunning Scottish scenery; delighted in the birds and the animals that allowed us to share their world for a moment; have learned how to watch the sky for weather patterns; have laughed and talked with the characters we met along the way; and above all, we have shared the whole experience together with joy.

We came back knowing where we belong, and what and who is important in our lives.

END – FIN – ENDE